Faith under Fire

Faith under Fire

33 DAYS OF
MISSILES AND MIRACLES

Eyewitness accounts and personal stories
of Israel's Northern War

Compiled and edited by
CHANA BESSER

A TARGUM PRESS Book

Published by:
TARGUM PRESS, INC.
22700 W. Eleven Mile Rd.
Southfield, MI 48034
E-mail: targum@targum.com
Fax: 888-298-9992
www.targum.com

Distributed by:
FELDHEIM PUBLISHERS
208 Airport Executive Park
Nanuet, NY 10954

Printing plates by Frank, Jerusalem
Printed in Israel by Chish

We are never alone. Everything we see and hear is reflective of Hashem's caring. The war seems far behind us because we like to stay in the immediate present. This is arguably the worst possible response to make to the fact that we were all in grave danger and saved by immense mercy. We must value our lives and the lives of our children far more than we do and imbue every day with as much meaning as we can.

Chana Besser's book is one of the best accounts of what life was like during the war. She records its spiritual history with the same sharp sense of moment-to-moment *hashgachah* as the physical diary of the events she lived through. Every day and every era is meant to teach us something new about our Infinite Master. She has succeeded in opening our eyes and our hearts.

Rebbetzin Tziporah Heller

This book is dedicated to
my daughters
Julie (Tova Rhya) Berman
and Cindy (Michal) Berman

and to my Rebbe,
HaRav Mordechai Dov Ber Twerski, *shlita*
The Hornosteipeler Rebbe

Contents

Preface 13
Foreword by Rabbi Mordechai Dov Ber Twerski 15

DISPATCHES FROM THE FRONT LINES:
THE WAR BEGINS

Chana Besser: Circle of Trust 21
Day 1 23
Day 2 27
Chana Besser: The First Shabbos 32
Chana Besser: Seven Years Ago This Parashah..............42

DISPATCHES FROM THE FRONT LINES:
LIVING WITH KATYUSHAS

Aharon Denton: No More Cereal..........................47
Day 4 49
Chana Besser: Katyusha Teshuvah 51
Day 5 56
Noga Dobkin: Update 61
Day 6 63
Chana Besser: Chickens 65
Adinah Rosen: Choose Life 67
Day 8 70
Rifca Goldberg: War Diary 72
Day 9 81

Chana Besser: The Second Shabbos under Fire 84

Day 10 88

Day 11 89

Day 12 99

Day 13 100

Chana Besser: Let's Respect Each Other's Decisions...... 103

THE REFUGEES

Chana Besser: Happy to Help................................... 111

Binyamin Alexander: Bus Terror............................. 114

Shira Yehudit Djlilmand: Diary of a War Refugee......... 116

Rebbetzin Tziporah Heller: To Stay or Not to Stay 122

Chana Besser: Blessing from Above
      (Hotel Rooms Down Below).................................. 125

Chava Rachel Saban: A Little of Our Story So Far 127

Johanna Yaffe: Excuses... 130

Esther Rubenstein: Listening with Your Heart............. 131

Esther Heller: "Is This a War, Mommy?"...................... 135

DISPATCHES FROM THE FRONT LINES: THE WAR CONTINUES

The Bostoner Rebbe Speaks about the War.................... 147

Rebbetzin Tziporah Heller: From Pizza to Teshuvah..... 151

Day 14 155

Chana Besser: Wartime Davening 157

Day 16 162

Chana Besser: A Step Closer to Geulah..................... 163

Day 18 165

Day 19 167

Day 21 169

Deborah Miller: Lamentation................................... 171

Day 23 173
Sarah Yehudit Schneider: Exploring the Question:
    How to Deal with Our Enemies 174
Day 25 176
Day 26 178
Shana Hovsha: Trip to the Shelters 179
Day 29 184
Bracha Adinah Denton: We Are All Crying.................188
Tuvia Natkin: Tzfat, August 2006 189
Day 33 190

THE ONES FIGHTING

Chana Besser: First Tefillin 193
Alida and Miles Bunder: On the Border.......................196
Rabbi Avraham Berkowitz: "Thank You for
    Your Protection" 200
Sue Tourkin-Komet: Noam 203
Roni Kadish: Unaware 205
Leiah Elbaum: Tishah B'Av in Her Voice.....................206

LOOKING BACK: THE AFTERMATH

Wendy Tikva Cohen: Hope for Life 214
A Letter of Thanks.......................................222
Chana Besser: Who Says You Don't
    Get a Second Chance?.................................... 225
Shira Yehudit Djlilmand: Before the War.....................231
Chana Besser: Rescued by Kindness.........................232
Chana Besser: Missiles and Miracles 239
Rabbi Dovid Heller: Finishing the Job 246

I Am Thankful To..249
Glossary...251

Preface

During the summer of 2006, the North of Israel was attacked from Lebanon. For thirty-three days, missiles rained down on the civilian population of Israel while Israeli soldiers fought in southern Lebanon and Gaza to defend us. Two million Israelis fled their homes or lived in bomb shelters. Tzefat, a small mountaintop town in the northern Galilee, was the third most shelled city in Israel, followed only by Kiryat Shemona and Nahariya.

Faith under Fire was written from the personal perspectives of the contributing writers. This is how each of us experienced the war. Much of the book was written in Tzefat during the war, sometimes as missiles were exploding. Some of the essays were written after the war.

These are our voices. They come from people who delivered meals under fire to shut-ins and elderly; from families confined to their homes or shelters; from those who had left the North, telling about their hardships and longing to come home; from people we never met, sending encouragement or writing about our soldiers. The anguish of the Jews in Melbourne or Seattle reverberates with the trauma of the Jews in Tzefat and Kiryat Shemona. In many instances, names have been changed upon request.

People will rightly say, "You didn't include the tremendous *chesed* done by So-and-so." This book contains only a small sampling of the oceans of *chesed* that poured out from Jews worldwide, especially from those in Israel who saw the need firsthand and were there to help. It includes only a small percentage of the bravery and *mesiras nefesh* that went on in our own town, and even less about the same throughout the North.

All over central and southern Israel, tens of thousands of families, yeshivahs, schools, factories, kibbutzes, *yishuvs*, and more gave or shared their housing, money, food, clothes, and toys, did laundry, and entertained the refugee familes from the North. Thousands of private individuals, shuls, and organizations worldwide raised money for Israel's soldiers and northern civilians. Many Jews dedicated their every waking moment and half their nights, stopping only for Shabbos. Non-Jews and millions of Jews opened their hearts and gave generously. This kept many alive, especially the grass-roots efforts that reached us while the need was dire. The stories in *Faith under Fire* will give the reader a glimpse of a few of these people.

The outpouring of love and prayers for our soldiers is poignantly touched upon in *Faith under Fire*. There is no way to count how many private citizens drove to the border during constant shelling to bring our soldiers gifts, encouragement, and basic necessities.

Let the personal stories presented in *Faith under Fire* be taken as a tribute to all. Be proud, *klal Yisrael*. Our enemies tried to defeat us. The way we took care of one another earned us the mercy of our Creator and brought us closer to the *geulah*.

Chana Besser
Shevat 5767

Foreword

BY RABBI MORDECHAI DOV BER TWERSKI, THE HORNOSTEIPELER REBBE

For many in the North of Israel, the summer of 2006, with Katyushas exploding in the fields and streets and buildings all around, felt like the end of days.

> *Vayehi miketz yamim...* — And it was at the end of days, Kayin brought from the fruit of the earth a *minchah* offering to Hashem. Hevel also brought from the first of his sheep and their fats; Hashem accepted Hevel and his *minchah*. But Kayin and his *minchah* He did not accept, and Kayin became angry and his face fell. Hashem asked Kayin: "What has caused you to anger and what has made your face fall?"
>
> *(Bereishis* 4:3–6)

The Kli Yakar points out the unique expression of *miketz yamim*, "the end of days." The Torah does not define which days and when. The Kli Yakar's explanation of this term adds an entire thought concept and insight into the parashah of Kayin and Hevel.

Miketz yamim represents the ultimate goal for which one strives. Kayin was *oved adamah*, a worker of the earth. He believed that the goal of one's accomplishments and the reward received from them were to be achieved and rewarded in this world, the world of the *adamah*. He rejected the goal of working for a purpose that is achieved only in the World to Come. Hevel, on the other hand, believed that life must yield a more spiritual result and chose the path of a shepherd for its meditative lifestyle of *hisbodedus* and the value of working with living souls, surpassing the materiality of this world.

Kayin and Hevel's disparate choices might also be interpreted in a similar fashion to the conflict between Yaakov and Esav. Yaakov strived to find that which is hidden inside the "tent" of this world, whereas Esav wanted the tangibility of the earthly fields. Kayin valued the rewards of this world and dedicated his life to making his perfected plot of *adamah* the goal of his service of Hashem. Hevel, on the other hand, disdained this world's acquisitions and saw this world as temporary and transitory.

This became the debate between these first brothers: What is the *ketz yamim*? What is the ultimate purpose of one's life?

Kayin presented his ultimate dedication to this world as an offering to his Creator, the fruits of the *adamah*; he offered Hashem his partnership in perfecting this material world. Hevel offered the life of the lambs that he shepherded; he offered Hashem his connection to the soul of this world as a demonstration of his dedication to the world of the *neshamah*, the soul. When Hashem accepted Hevel's offering, Kayin saw it as the total rejection of his life's efforts and goals. He challenged Hashem with anger at this rejection of what had become his primary goal. Hashem then challenged Kayin to reexamine his priorities:

> If you will improve yourself, mistakes can be tolerated; however, if you do not strive to improve your purpose, the door leads you toward the path of error.
>
> *(Bereishis 4:7)*

Kayin challenged Hevel to debate these values. If Hevel truly believed that the material is ultimately insignificant, would he tolerate suffering in this world, since the real value of one's efforts is for spiritual wholeness rather than physical comfort? Hevel responded that the *sadeh*, the "field" representing the physical world, is only temporary and that physical pain is transitory. Kayin struck out at him, wounding him repeatedly, in disbelief that Hevel would tolerate physical suffering for belief in the World to Come. Kayin taunted Hevel, "Will you be willing to give up your life for your belief in the world of the *neshamah*?" Still Hevel clung firmly to the premise that even physical death is not a deterrent to the ultimate purpose of the path of the *neshamah*. He confronted Kayin with the choice of the wrongfulness caused by inflicting harm on another in spite of the rebuke that Hashem had given Kayin.

> Kayin spoke with his brother Hevel. And it happened, when they were in the field, that Kayin rose up against his brother Hevel and killed him. Hashem said to Kayin, "Where is Hevel your brother?" And he said, "I do not know. Am I my brother's keeper?"
>
> (*Bereishis* 4:8–9)

Kayin fulfilled his challenge to Hevel of the ultimate test of the *ketz yamim*, the cost of his life for belief in the World to Come. Upon seeing the death of his brother, Kayin began to doubt his faith in the materiality of the world. Hashem reached out to Kayin in his confusion and asked him, "Kayin, where is your brother now? If there is no other world beyond this, where is his soul now?" Kayin struggled to find the answer with the denial of his responsibility for his brother's choice of death rather than turn away from his beliefs. Hashem opened Kayin's ears to hear the consequence of these actions:

> Your brother's blood cries out to Me from the *adamah*! Therefore...when you work the ground, it shall no longer yield its strength to you. You shall become a vagrant and a wanderer on earth.
>
> (*Bereishis* 4:10–11)

The physical world cannot hold back the cry of your brother's pain and death, Hashem told Kayin. There must be another level of existence beyond this world. You have chosen your attachment to the material world, and so you will suffer the consequence of being its prisoner for all time; you will be a wanderer of the earth forever. Kayin came to the realization that his beliefs were in error:

> *Gadol avoni minso...* My sin is too great to bear... Can I be hidden from Your Presence?
>
> (Bereishis 4:13–14)

Kayin now understood the full impact of his *ketz yamim*, of having lived his life with only this world before him. "I now see," he said, "that I have not only lost any value of this world, but I have lost the ability to see Your Face, to have a greater awareness of an infinite Creator." Hashem then commuted the sentence to seven generations so that Kayin could live to see the development of mankind toward a greater *ketz yamim*: spiritual eternity, that which ascends beyond the limitations of the material world.

The summer of 2006 in the North of Israel was one of the many times that *klal Yisrael* has suffered the pain and tragedy of this ongoing struggle with the Kayins and the Esavs of the world. Our brothers' blood was literally being spilled around us. Even though we were bleeding, we were mourning, we were in trauma, *klal Yisrael* did not lose sight of our higher purpose. We can even say that in many instances it was because of our suffering that *klal Yisrael* found our higher purpose. This is clearly evident in so many of the beautifully told stories that are shared in this book. We daven that there will come a time soon when the Kayins and the Esavs of the world will also recognize the higher purpose to which *klal Yisrael* dedicates itself, when the world will be united as one in the true *ketz hayamim*.

The War Begins

Faith under Fire

CHANA BESSER

Circle of Trust

Thursday, July 13, 2006
17 Tammuz 5766

"Look at that fire!"

"Where?"

"There, about halfway up Mount Meron, beyond Rabbi Shimon's *kever*."

"Do you think it was started by a missile?"

"Don't know. Could be."

"They're aiming for that army base on the top of the mountain."

"I hear one."

"Me, too."

They were distant. An inexperienced ear would take them for sonic booms. But we knew better. Mount Meron was being shelled.

The five of us exchanged solemn glances. We had taken a calculated risk driving to the grave site of the *navi* Chavakuk. It was Rabbi Hoffman's annual Tzefat visit for his yearly Torah seminar, and we always went to the *kevarim* with him to study the Torah of the tzaddikim buried there. War was going to break out any moment. We knew that. The question was whether they would shell Tzefat. They had never shelled Tzefat before in any of Israel's wars, but ever since Israel's withdrawal from Lebanon, we knew Tzefat was well within firing range.

Early in the afternoon of a hot, summer fast day, the seventeenth of Tammuz, the first missiles exploded the serenity of the mystical mountaintop town of Tzefat.

A few of us wound up in the same bomb shelter. "What are you thinking about?" I asked Rabbi Hoffman.

"Why did I witness the first shot of both wars?" he said. "I was in Jerusalem in 1967 and saw the first shot of the Six-Day War. Now I'm seeing the first shot on Tzefat, the seventeenth of Tammuz. The Ba'al Shem Tov says we have to ask why we see what we see."

Silence.

"So, Chana, what did you learn from Chavakuk's circle drawings?"

At Chavakuk's *kever*, Rabbi Hoffman had taught that safety is a personal relationship with Hashem. We learn to draw a circle of trust that keeps us safe even in the middle of a bombardment. As the prophet said, "I will stand at my watchtower and station myself on my rampart; I will keep watch to see what He will say to me, and what He will answer concerning my complaint" (*Chavakuk* 2:1).

"I'm working on it. Right now, I'm not drawing much of a circle around me. To tell the truth, I'm trusting more in the thickness of these bomb shelter walls."

"Maybe that's why we're here. So that we can each work on drawing our circle."

CHANA BESSER was born in a displaced persons' camp in post–World War II Europe. She grew up in Chicago, raised two daughters in Denver, traveled around the world, and then made aliyah to Tzefat, in 1995. Her short stories and articles have appeared in *Horizons, Heartbeats II, Hamodia, The Jewish Tribune of London,* and other Jewish publications.

Day 1

Date: July 13, 2006
From: Chana Besser
To: Tzefat under Fire list
Subject: I'm OK — we've been bombed

Tzefat was hit hard this afternoon, several direct hits from Lebanon. Some people ended up in the hospital.

They shoot Katyushas, small rockets. Each one can take out a room or a good hunk of a room. If it lands just so, it could bring down a small house. Windows can break for up to two blocks away.

The Old City was hit hard in the first round on this first day of the war. People ran for bomb shelters that hadn't been used in years. Many were padlocked. The locks were quickly broken. Peter Mond, a friend and neighbor, opened one of them and then patrolled the neighborhood, one of the few who stayed out on the streets to tell people where the shelters were.

People are slowly coming out on the streets again, but ready to run inside on a moment's notice. We are still fasting, saying a lot of te-hillim — you can, too, for us and for everybody. I can't tell you if it's over yet. I can tell you that people are handling it very, very well.

kol tuv, chana

Date: July 13, 2006
From: Sue Tourkin-Komet
To: Chana Besser
Subject: Re: I'm OK — we've been bombed

Just one tiny "tikkun" — when you are being shelled, by katyushot, that's the word: shelled. Altho' you may certainly FEEL like you are being "bombed," as such a slight difference in wording is more than slight. (I've lived thru wars in Israel nonstop since 1968, so my vocabulary of war-like proper terms exists in Hebrew and in English...)

Shells come from a certain distance, even a long distance, over borders, sailing towards their final destination, sideways — almost horizontally. Bombs come from above, from overhead, vertically, from aerial bombing, meaning the enemy's aircraft is flying right over your head[s], chas v'shalom.

Or bombs come from suicide/homicide bombers. No need to elaborate too much on what that means.

So please take care.

I think that after we (in Gilo) had two years (2000-2002) of day and night gunfire and missiles (mortar shells) hitting us from The Enemy in Beit Jalla, I have a little bit too much experience in such areas.

I do not write this glibly. I write it with a shakiness and a lump in my guts and a lump in my throat and held-back tears, bitter tears. I can taste those tears in my throat, oh yes I can taste bitter tears.

Luv, sue

Date: July 13, 2006
From: Chana Besser
To: Tzefat under Fire list
Subject: Music in the miklat

We had a few hours of quiet late in the afternoon, and then early evening we were heavily shelled again. They scored at least two or three more direct hits in town. I'm OK, all my friends are OK. But there are some people seriously injured. Most of the people showing up at the hospital are there for shock and light shrapnel wounds. The majority are walking out of the hospital right after their treatment. But I'm worried about the people who were badly hurt.

I had a lovely break-the-fast meal in the bomb shelter, brought in by Muriel Chefetz. She lives next door to the shelter and has a large, beautiful family, bli ayin hara. Muriel cooked earlier in the day amidst the then distant shelling. This evening her family sang together to allay the children's fears. Others joined in.

A few ragged-looking young hippies walked into the shelter with their musical instruments. The Klezmer Festival had just ended two nights before the first missile hit Tzefat. Evidently, these young people never left town after Klezmer. Can you imagine the injuries and pandemonium if the town would have been full of tens of thousands of music festival visitors? Another sign of our Creator's love for us.

Holding a musical instrument case, a tall, thin, unkempt, long-haired young man dressed in loose-fitting, white cotton clothes stood in the doorway, smiling at the scene of Muriel with two children on her lap and another two snuggling up against her, one on either side of her chair. The children were singing what has become the theme song from Gush Katif, very appropriate for today, beseeching Hashem not to turn away from us.

The more they sang, the more the children relaxed and the wider the young man smiled. His face was aglow. For sure he'll be a ba'al teshuvah from this, I thought to myself. But did Hashem have to bring a war to do it?

It's late and I'm home now. Don't worry — if I hear any activity, I'll be right back in that shelter for the night. It's down my street.

If it's scary tonight or in the morning, I'll leave for Shabbos. The roads are open. Don't worry. I'm fine. Really.

kol tuv, chana

Date: July 13, 2006
From: Chana Besser
To: Tzefat under Fire list
Subject: Casualties of our first day under attack

We lost our first Jewish life. Baruch Dayan ha'emes. And a whole family is injured. It's a bloody first day. Nitzan Rozban, age 33, was riding a bicycle when a Katyusha struck near the Macabi Health Clinic in the Artists' Quarter.

This afternoon, just around sunset, close to the end of the fast day, a family of seven was seriously injured when a Katyusha hit their apartment. It's the building with the wooden pelican in a tuxedo sitting above the green gate.

One of the children was quickly airlifted to Rambam Hospital. She was unconscious by then.

From Hamodia newspaper:

"The public was asked to daven for four children...injured in the attack on Tzefat...

Michal bat Revital

Bat-Tzion bat Revital

Odel Chana bat Revital

Avraham Natan ben Revital."

That's the end of the Hamodia article. We should be davening for the mother, too.

Home of the family of seven struck on the first day of the war

Day 2

Date: July 14, 2006
From: Chana Besser
To: Tzefat under Fire list
Subject: Good morning...it's still quiet here — for now

Morning and all is well at 9:30 a.m.!

The bakeries, groceries, and a few essential shops are open. Some people are out and about getting ready for Shabbos. Our airplanes buzz overhead, another one almost every two minutes, and people here are trying to consolidate the rumors and get an accurate accounting of who was hurt (may they be healed) and where exactly we were shelled.

We are not getting any updates on the few people who were seriously injured, nor do I know any of their names. Most of the media are reporting that a new Ethiopian immigrant was wounded. I don't think he was seriously hurt.

It seems like there were a few hits in the Canaan neighborhood and one or two struck homes or courtyards of homes.

Most of the Katyushas didn't hurt anybody, baruch Hashem. But they were plenty close and striking all over town. A good portion of our residents fled yesterday to Tiveria or further South, and they will probably not come back until after Shabbos. B'ezras Hashem, it should stay quiet and safe.

I couldn't fall asleep last night till after my landlord's rooster crowed. His first crowing is at 4:35 a.m. I taped up my bedroom windows, laid my dressing mirror on the floor under the wardrobe, and pushed my bed all the way into the nook near the door to prevent getting hurt, chas v'shalom, by the wardrobe falling on me or by flying glass. Processing all that had happened in our sleepy little town, known until today as one of the safest places in Israel, made sleep impossible until almost dawn. I guess I'll daven now and get a cup of coffee.

Thank you for all the e-mails and phone calls of encouragement, support, and prayers from outside of town and from outside of Israel and for the many Shabbos invitations. Forgive me for not writing to each of you personally.

The silver lining to the cloud is that all of us Jews are together on the same side now, and we are all united against an evil enemy who is external to the Jewish people. That feels good and does much in the heavens above to protect us. The Kosel is crowded this morning with Jews praying for Jews. I saw it on the Aish.com website. It gives me much strength.

Please continue your prayers and good deeds and tzedakah, because although Tzefat is quiet as of this writing, other Yidden are in danger and our soldiers need us!

kol tuv, chana

Date: July 14, 2006
From: Chana Besser
To: Tzefat under Fire list
Subject: Miracles

I called my friend.

"Sara, I heard there were some explosions in the Givat Shoshana neighborhood Thursday. Are you and your family all right?"

"Yes, my son's courtyard was hit, right across the street from me. And they are all fine, baruch Hashem. Their windows broke. That's all."

"Baruch Hashem!"

I was speaking with Rebbetzin Sara Kaplan and she was telling me about her son, Rabbi Chaim Kaplan, and his wife and family.

"Wait, that's not the end of the story," she said. "They told him to go to the city building and file a report so that he would be reimbursed for the repairs. So a few hours later, he gets in his car and he is driving into town, and just as he is approaching the traffic circle by the Bezek building, a missile explodes near his car. All but two of his car's windows broke, and he was covered with broken glass. Only one piece of shrapnel flew at him, and it didn't hurt him because it hit him on the shoulder pad of his suit jacket. But the glass cut his nose and hands and slivers of glass got in his eyes.

"He got out of his car bleeding and hitched a ride to the hospital. They got all the glass out of his eyes, gave him a few stitches on his nose, bandaged up his hands, and sent him home. He's fine. When you think of what could have happened, it was a day of open miracles."

Date: July 14, 2006
From: Chana Besser
To: Tzefat under Fire list
Subject: Like the Inquisition

I spent the scary part of the morning in the bomb shelter and came home at a quiet time to get ready for Shabbos. Then I was afraid to shower.

Lichvod Shabbos kodesh, I told myself. In honor of the holy Shabbos. Chana, "lishmor nafshoseichem me'od" (taking VERY careful care of your lives) is also a mitzvah. The Torah says "Shamor Shabbos" — it doesn't say "me'od..." ("Keep the Shabbos," but not "Keep the Shabbos very much").

That was my internal dialogue. Then I remembered the mesiras nefesh of the Spanish Jews. Before the Inquisition, a Jew was given the death sentence in Spain if a neighbor testified that he had seen smoke coming out of the Jew's chimney on a Friday. Why? Because Jews always bathed to prepare for the Shabbos on Friday before sunset, and they had to boil up buckets full of water for their pre-Shabbos baths, requiring a fire to heat the water, and smoke from the fire came out of their chimneys.

It always brought tears to my eyes when I'd think of how they risked their lives to bathe "lichvod Shabbos kodesh."

Well, I'm not risking my life — much. Nobody's going to execute me in any Inquisition today. My odds of surviving are excellent. I haven't heard any shelling for a few hours. So at my level, this is my gesture of a teeny-tiny bit of mesiras nefesh for Hashem, for a little lady who's not at the level of those Spanish Jews but nevertheless inspired by them. We take small steps.

I survived the shower, dressed appropriately for the holy Shabbos, and had not much else to do in the way of honoring the holy Sabbath. I'll either spend it in a bomb shelter with the food that I have already cooked or go to a family on the block for the meals, if it is very quiet. It depends on the level of alert when Shabbos comes in tonight.

• • •

Prayers Requested on Behalf of Hostage Soldiers

(IsraelNN.com) Rabbis are calling on Jews around the world to recite a special prayer for those Israelis in danger in areas within rocket range, both in northern and southern Israel.

In addition, as women light Sabbath candles, they are requested to recite a special prayer for the hostaged soldiers:

Gilad ben Aviva (Shalit)

Eldad ben Tova (Regev)

Ehud ben Malka (Goldwasser)

Missile sticking out of the ground that struck near the Macabi Clinic, killing a man

CHANA BESSER

The First Shabbos

Shabbos, July 15, 2006
19 Tammuz 5766

There was a mass exodus on Friday. Cars, taxis, buses were filled, all going one way, the opposite direction of every other Shabbos of the year.

By now, those of us left in Tzefat were not as scared as we had been on Thursday. In the last couple of days we have become war-wise. The little *pop pops* from a distance and *boom booms* from closer — but not close enough to be threatening — have become background noise.

We know that if a Katyusha is close enough, we will hear a screechy whistley sound for at least a minute as a warning. If we don't hear the screechy whistle, it will land somewhere else. So far, I've heard it about three or four times.

"All of your Shabbos guests have left Tzefat, and I might not come either if Katyushas are flying," I had told Hadassah on Thursday night.

"Well, if you come, we'll be in the Ohel Avraham bomb shelter. You can join us there."

"Chana, come over and eat with us." It was Elisheva on the telephone. "For both meals."

It was a welcome invitation — if I had the courage to dash

down the street. (They lived only a block away.)

"If they aren't shelling, I'll come. But it might not be safe to leave. This time, don't wait for me for Kiddush." They always waited. "I mean it. Because I'm not leaving the house if there are Katyushas. I have food. I'm just coming for the company."

The usual Shabbos sirens to signal candle-lighting time weren't sounded. It was wise not to sound them. They are the same sirens used for air-raid alerts.

I lit my Shabbos candles and started my Shabbos prayers alone at home. Few men were walking to shul down my street. Usually hundreds of residents and tourists pass on their way to all the famous synogogues in the Old City, many of them singing. People who never sing on the streets in their own hometown sing when they walk down the streets in Tzefat on Shabbos. Only one lone man was singing Shabbos songs outside. Every few minutes another man or two would scurry by. Outside my kitchen window, overlooking Gan HaKasum, a Breslov chassid strolled slowly and happily down the street, conversing with his three little sons, as if it were an ordinary Shabbos. But not another soul was in sight. The emptiness of Tzefat on a Shabbos night at candle-lighting time was eerie.

In the middle of my *Kabbalas Shabbos* prayers, the air-raid siren sounded, long and loud and insistently. The sky was just going dark. I grabbed my prepared emergency Shabbos kit sitting beside the front door — a little canvas sack with a siddur, *sefer Tehillim*, lots of Kleenex, my I.D. card, an apple and a banana, and a thin sweater. Next to it was a bottle of water and my house keys. I ran, my heart pounding, passing the first shelter across from the Sanzer Shul. I wasn't going to a private home for this meal.

An ambulance with the engine running stood in front of the Sanzer Shul. A chassid stood outside of it. "The shelter is just a few meters ahead," he said in Hebrew.

"I know, thanks," I answered, not breaking my stride. *Whew! Baruch Hashem, nothing has exploded.*

I ran down the shelter steps, hoping to be with the same wonderful people who had been there on Thursday. No one was inside. I walked through all three rooms — the little back room, the medium-sized entry room, and the large *kollel* room beside it. No one. This was not going to be a fun Shabbos. Then I remembered that I hadn't taken my food out of the refrigerator. I hadn't brought a bottle of wine or grape juice on purpose. Running in the street with glass in your hands isn't a smart thing to do.

A huge explosion went off, the loudest I had ever heard. Even inside the shelter it was very loud, but the walls didn't shake underground.

I guess it's safe down here. Another loud explosion. I waited. Quiet. We know now that if it is quiet for a while after a series of blasts, the enemy needs time to run to a new place and set up again before he is spotted. That's when it is safe to dash out if necessary. Sometimes we get a break for a couple hours, but usually it is a shorter interval of quiet. Good. I could finish my davening.

No booms disturbed my *Shemoneh Esrei*. The next order of business was Kiddush and *hamotzi* if it was still quiet.

I walked upstairs and stood right next to the door of the bomb shelter, afraid to take more than a step or two from the entrance. Yitzchak, an American local, came walking by just as an ambulance pulled up. I heard him briefing the ambulance driver.

"One exploded in an empty field, just downhill a bit from Ari Street, and the other one has injuries," he shouted to the ambulance. "A family was hurt in the Old City. A Katyusha hit a house on that narrow pathway below Chernobyl Shul, going toward Jerusalem Street." They'll have to go in on foot or motorcyle. That cobblestone street isn't wide enough to drive a car down, and there's a staircase at both ends of it.

Every few minutes a man would walk by, going to shul or coming back from shul to check on his family.

The town drunk had staggered down the street during the commotion with the ambulance. Yitzchak handled him well, calming him down. He didn't look frightened and didn't have enough command of himself to know he should seek cover.

"If you look at me, you'll have sons," he told me. "I'm Mashiach."

Mashiach would know that I'm not married and have had all the children I'll ever have, I thought.

We get a lot of people coming through Tzefat who think they are Mashiach. Once, a young lady went to a *mekubal* in Tzefat to ask his advice about a young man she was seeing on *shidduch*. "He's perfect in every way except for one thing that bothers me. He thinks he is Mashiach."

The *mekubal* gave her his beautiful smile filled with patience and compassion. "Yes, I just had three others come to me this week, all thinking they were Mashiach." In his sweet, soft, fatherly way, he suggested she find someone normal.

Tonight's Mashiach staggered down the road with Yitzchak. But when Yitzchak continued on, the poor, broken soul turned around. I dashed inside the shelter. He was headed my way. Being alone with a drunk man in a bomb shelter was not my idea of *oneg Shabbos*.

He's not coming into the shelter. If he wanted to be inside, he wouldn't be out on the streets, I told myself. Mashiach staggered past, shouting whatever he was shouting, and slowly disappeared down the street.

Two chassidim walked by. "I don't have any wine and I don't have any challah!" I shouted. "Do you live nearby?"

One nodded. "Yes."

"Can you bring me some?" I asked.

He nodded again.

Ten minutes went by. *Their wives aren't letting them out*, I figured.

I waited some more. The night air was lovely. Someone would come by.

"*Git Shabbos*," I greeted a woman who came out on her balcony nearby for a dangerous moment of fresh air. I had never met her.

"*Gut Shabbos*," she returned.

"I don't have any wine, and I don't have any challah," I said in Hebrew.

"Come eat with us," she answered in English. They always do

that as soon as they hear my accent.

I didn't answer. It was a top-floor apartment with a flat roof. My house was safer than that.

"We have a safe room," she added.

"OK, I'm coming!"

Big smiles and a warm welcome greeted me while their big-eyed children stared at their unexpected wartime guest like Eliyahu HaNavi.

"Where did you make aliyah from?" Yisrael asked.

"Denver."

"Do you know Motti Twerski?" asked Chana. We were both named Chana.

"The Rebbe of Hornosteipel, Rav Mordechai Twerski, *shlita*, is my Rebbe!"

"You're kidding! I lived in their home. He *'mekareved'* me!"

"But you're an Israeli. How did you wind up in Denver?" I asked.

"I was living in Colorado Springs, and Shlomo Carlebach came through. He took me to Motti Twerski's house in Denver and left me there. I became their bas bayis."

Thank you, Rebbe, for davening for me. I thought. *And for sending me your bas bayis with a Shabbos meal. I only asked Hashem for wine and challah.*

I stayed for the whole Shabbos meal — the usual eight or more Israeli salads and three more courses, served leisurely, as if there were nothing unusual about this first Shabbos of the war. The men sang all the Shabbos *zemiros*. But every time a boom sounded, Chana flinched.

ଔ ଔ ଔ

What's that? I asked myself, partly awakened by *pop-popping* noises from afar before dawn. *Oh, yeah, we're at war.* I went back to sleep. I had decided to sleep in my own bed, pushed far away from the window. "Those arched ceilings make your home as strong as any bomb shelter," I had been told.

"Shabbos," I whispered.

Around 11:00 a.m. was one of those quiet times. I dashed down the block to Elisheva's house. The street was empty, but there was strong, joyful singing, many men's voices. It was coming from the Tzemach Tzaddik Chabad Shul near Kikar Maginim. On the way I could see the damage from the Katyusha that had fallen close to the Chernobyl Shul. There was a hole in the middle of the tiled courtyard.

Hey, it's not so big, I told myself. My fear index went way down. I had imagined much more damage. This was a hole about six to eight inches deep and ten to twelve inches in diameter. The courtyard was full of rubble from plants and debris.

When we arrived, we all sat down to lunch. "Are you going to stay in town?" Elisheva asked, offering more sweet potatoes and vegetarian cholent.

"I'm not so scared. Only when they come really close," I admitted. "When I feel scared, I'll leave. For now, I'm fine."

"A Jew shouldn't make decisions based on their feelings," said her husband, a *rosh kollel*. He always dressed in white on Shabbos. "Feelings can be misleading. A Jew makes decisions according to the Torah. Rav Auerbach, *z"tl*, came out very strongly against Jews making decisions based solely on their feelings."

Best to change the subject. "Oh, you have leechi nuts! I can say a *shehecheyanu!*" It was my second *shehecheyanu* this Shabbos. I had also worn a new blouse. Anything that would increase the joy of Shabbos was a *kiddush Hashem* now.

They walked me part of the way home during a quiet time. We went just half a block out of our way via the street below to see the street where three buildings had been hit. One of the less damaged buildings was the Tschortkop Shul. The place was filled with dust and debris, but the ark was untouched, not a scratch on it. The western door was blown off its hinges, but all the holy books had been untouched on the northern wall. Not a book was out of place.

The Tschortkop Shul is surrounded by three other popular shuls, each within fifty feet — Chernobyl, Makarev, and Vizhnitz-Tunis. On Shabbos there is standing room only. But last night the men had gathered in the Ari Shul to make a minyan. No one was in the Tschortkop Shul when the Katyusha struck it. Another sign of Hashem's kindness, even in the midst of His acts of strict judgment.

଼ ଼ ଼

It was still quiet when I got to Kikar Maginim near my home. Rabbi Shmuel Eliyahu, the chief rabbi of Tzefat, was standing outside the bomb shelter in the square, almost directly across the street from his house.

"*Shabbat shalom,*" I greeted him. I knew he wouldn't initiate a greeting to a woman on the street, but I also knew that he would answer me if I greeted him first. What good is a war if you can't take a little advantage?

"*Shabbat shalom.*"

I'm very forunate to have such holy neighbors. Rabbi Eliyahu's family lives on one side of the health food store, and Rabbi Elazar Koenig lives on the other side of it. Both of them are very powerful men spiritually. Rabbi Eliyahu saved a family's life a year ago on Sukkos, when her family lived across the cobblestone path from the *rav.* A wiring fault in their refrigerator caused a fire Sukkos morning when almost all the men were in shul davening. Rabbi Eliyahu davens at sunrise, so he was home already. When he went outside, all the neighbors were frantically trying to break open a window or the front door. The family was locked inside — the children had played with the key, and they couldn't find it. Meanwhile the fire spread and the smoke thickened. The children were screaming, and their mother could not succeed in putting the fire out.

Rabbi Eliyahu walked up to the locked front door and opened it. He didn't break it. He opened it. Without a key. He got the family out with all the kids on the sidewalk in their pajamas.

"Rebbetzin, is it true that your husband opened that door on Sukkos during the fire?" I asked his wife one Shabbos months later. We both knew everyone had tried to open that door and they couldn't. She smiled. I guess you learn a few tricks when your

Hole made by a missile that struck the Me'or Chaim neighborhood of Tzefat

father was one of the chief *gabbaim* of the Baba Sali.

He wouldn't need to use any special powers today, G-d willing. The shelter doors were wide open.

ᔥ ᔥ ᔥ

"Chana, how are you?"

It was the Trabelsi family calling after Shabbos.

"Come and stay with us. We have room for you."

"No, I'm fine here. Thanks, I'm staying in Tzefat."

"Well, if you are staying, then will you feed Yochai's chickens?"

"Feed the chickens?"

"Yes, feed the chickens."

"I don't know how to feed chickens. I'm a city kid. I grew up in Chicago."

"They eat everything. Just give them leftovers and water every day."

I remembered that somebody had asked Rebbetzin Tzipora Heller how we can know whether we should say yes or no when we are offered a chesed or a mitzvah. Rebbetzin Heller advised, as I remember it, that most of the time, we should do what we do well, what we are comfortable doing. But we should also stretch a little. We don't have to go looking for it, but when something that doesn't suit us comes across our path, and Hashem offers us a mitzvah or a chesed, then that is a sign that we should do it. Don't walk away from it if it comes to you.

Well, Rebbetzin Heller, thanks. I'll be thinking of you every day when I feed my landlord's chickens.

That rooster has irritated me since it found its voice. It crows at a little after four in the morning from a few feet outside my bedroom window. Then it crows almost every hour. I complained once and grumbled almost every day to myself. The message was obvious.

OK, Hashem. I'll take care of the chickens. It's a lesson for me not to bear a grudge. But did You have to bring a war for me to learn it?

To my landlord, I said, "Sure, I'll feed them."

The phone rang again. "Chana, this was the greatest Shabbos of my life."

Rivka Michal had been in her safe room with her three-year-old daughter and three guests — Feigi, who lives in her building, Feigi's daughter, and her son-in-law.

"Little Chana Yehudit was thrilled. To her, this is just one big pajama party. Shabbos afternoon the four little kids next door came over to play. They're from three to eight years old. When the littler ones got scared by the booms, the older ones starting singing. At first their singing was faint, but then they all joined in together and all of the kids were singing with all of their might: 'V'ha'ikar v'ha'ikar lo lefacheid lo lefacheid klal... — The whole world is a very narrow bridge, and the most important thing is not to be afraid at all.'

"They started dancing and singing and shouting out the words — they chased the fear right out of themselves. The beauty of it was that no adult initiated or encouraged it. As young as they were, they already knew how to connect with our Creator when He seems the farthest away."

Lots of phone calls after Shabbos — everyone was checking on everyone. From what we had all heard, it appeared that no one had been hurt in our town in all the shelling on Shabbos.

"*Shavua tov,*" we blessed each other. That night the words took on new meaning.

This essay was first published in *Hamodia* weekly newspaper.

CHANA BESSER

Seven Years Ago
This Parashah

Motza'ei Shabbos, July 15, 2006
15 Tammuz 5766

For those who had remained in Tzefat to face the first Shabbos under missile fire, it was very brave of any man, and a few women, to venture forth to shul to make a minyan. And yet many minyanim were held. For Yehuda, perhaps the decision to go to shul was braver than for others.

Seven years ago on this Shabbos, *parashas Pinchas*, Yehuda had been shot walking to shul on Friday night. An anti-Semitic gunman looking for Jews to kill had driven to West Rogers Park, a religious Jewish neighborhood of Chicago, and opened fire. He had wounded some Jews already, pulling up next to them and shooting from inside his car as they walked to shul. Yehuda and two of his daughters heard the shots, but it was the Fourth of July. "Firecrackers," he told them.

The gunman drove up next to Yehuda, opened fire, and shot twelve bullets at very close range. Only one bullet out of the twelve hit him, in itself a wonder considering how close the gunman was. Sadly, we know the gunman was a very good shot. He drove to another neighborhood, Skokie, took one shot from much further away, and killed a non-Jew walking down the street.

The doctors couldn't find any trace of the bullet in Yehuda. It had entered his body, gone through two layers of skin, and then disappeared. The doctor, not inclined to believe in disappearing bullets, concluded that the bullet had backed out through the same hole it had entered. When asked how a bullet does such a thing when flesh does not offer much resistance to a bullet, the doctor had no answer.

"Should I *bentch gomel*?" Yehuda had asked his *rav*. The *rav* asked his *rav*, a *gadol* in Eretz Yisrael. The *pesak* came back: "No."

Gray cloud rising from a missile strike on the Canaan neighborhood of Tzefat

There was no need to *bentch gomel*, because Yehuda was never in danger. It was a revealed miracle.

"Are you sure you want to walk out there tonight, with missiles exploding so close by, considering what happened seven years ago on this parashah?" his wife asked, more than a little worried.

"The *rav* said the Master of the world is in control here just as much as He is anywhere else," Yehuda said. "I'm going to shul."

DISPATCHES FROM THE FRONT LINES

Living with Katyushas

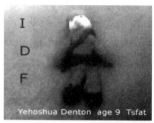

Yehoshua Denton's clay soldier

AHARON DENTON

No More Cereal

Sunday, July 16, 2006
20 Tammuz 5766

It was not an ordinary Thursday when I stood with my family in our kitchen in the Old City of Tzefat. Katyusha rockets had already begun striking several cities in the north on Wednesday. We could hear and see them as they landed across the valley on Mount Meron. Nothing could have prepared us for what happened next.

My wife, oldest daughter, and I were standing in our kitchen. They were eating cereal at around three o'clock, when from out of nowhere, *ka-boom! KA-BOOM!* Then came the sound of a jet streaking across the sky, but it became quickly apparent that it was not a jet. A loud whistling noise followed. I stood there, watching this thing streak across the sky from our kitchen window, slamming into the mountain next to the marble-cutting factory on Ari Street.

KA-BOOM! Cereal everywhere! It was all over the table, floor, counter, ceiling, and wall. *Oy vey*, what a mess! We decided it was best to stay in the safe room after that.

By Friday night, all seven of our scheduled guests had left town, and it was only my family sitting at a small portable Shabbos table in our apartment's safe room. We finished the fish course along with some distant booms outside, and I cautiously went to the kitchen. I was standing at our window, looking at Mount Meron, when I saw some lights coming from the west and then that already familiar sound of *ka-boom KA-BOOM*.

My wife was yelling my name. I turned around toward her and headed for the safe room as an incoming rocket headed for us, but there was no time. *KA-BOOM!*

A rocket exploded about twenty yards from where I was standing, ten yards from the balcony between our house and the next house. A huge flash of fire burst forth at the back of the building. *Baruch Hashem*, no windows were broken in our building, and only one window in the building beside ours. This was too close.

Shabbos and Sunday thankfully saw no other close calls. We decided to have breakfast in the hallway next to the safe room on our portable table. On the menu: cereal. Cooking pancakes or eggs in the middle of a war, in a place where a rocket lands only twenty meters from you, is probably not a good idea. Three kids had finished eating and already returned to the safe room after spilling a bowl of milk on the floor (which would come in handy a minute later). I had just walked in from the balcony when that now familiar sound scorched the air.

"GET DOWN!" I yelled as my wife ran toward the table to get our three-year-old, who was sitting comfortably at the table eating her cereal. My wife slipped on the spilled milk and slid to the floor, but skillfully took the cereal-eating three-year-old with her.

I didn't make it to the safe room. I stopped in my tracks just inside the balcony door, waiting for the *KA-BOOM!* and the feeling of shards of shrapnel piercing my body. Thankfully, for us anyway, the missile went screaming over the top of our building and hit some unknown place about 150 yards away. As everyone in the family began to recover, I had only one thing to say: "It is now forbidden to eat cereal in this house!"

AHARON DENTON made aliyah from America to Tzefat with his wife, Bracha Adinah, and their five children in July 2003.

Day 4

We have Tzefat families who would leave town, but they have no bus fare. And there are families who are staying, but they are out of food money. I'm collecting for them.

Chana

• • •

Date: July 16, 2006
From: Chana Besser
To: Tzefat under Fire list
Subject: Update

As of almost 8 p.m., a much quieter day, baruch Hashem. Especially quieter in the afternoon. No injuries that I have heard of. I'm afraid our relative quiet in Tzefat is at the expense of Haifa.

The grocery stores in the Old City are stocked with plenty of the basics. Newspapers are available. The garbage was collected. Is the post office open in town? Is there mail delivery? I'm not going out there to find out.

I'm asking everyone to take extra precautions about how we say things when we give over information to others. The tension and stress interferes with our brain's ability to process what we hear. I am sitting inside my house with nice thick walls. I'm not running around on the streets wearing a hard hat, documenting what people tell me.

There was a rumor that Kalman was killed by the missile that hit near the Macabi clinic. I called his friend. Kalman is alive and well, baruch Hashem. His friend saw the man hurt on the pavement. He said it wasn't Kalman, but that he certainly looked a lot like Kalman from afar.

Later I saw Kalman, and he told me he was there at the scene, standing next to the man who was hurt and that the man was later niftar. By the next day, there were some very disturbed friends of Kalman trying to find his levayah, and one friend even went to Kalman's house to pay a shivah call. Imagine his surprise to find Kalman home, alive and well! They say it is a segulah for a long life if people say in error that you have died, so may Kalman live to 120 in good health!

chana

CHANA BESSER

Katyusha Teshuvah

Monday, July 17, 2006
21 Tammuz 5766

The Katyusha missile exploded while I was standing in my kitchen in Tzefat looking out the window at the view of Mount Meron and the hills of the Galilee.

"I'll call you back!" I hung up on my friend, who had taken her family out of town after their own two close encounters with Katyushas.

Raw power. My heart pounded. My knees turned to jelly. Instant fear, but too late to do anything about it. The missile was louder than any thunder bolt, louder than ten thunder bolts.

I'm OK, I realized. *It didn't even break my windows. How is that possible? That had to be next door.*

Then quiet. I waited a few minutes. Except for a fast pulse, my body had returned to normal. I had to find out where that missile had exploded. I cautiously left my house. Moments later, I found it. It was a few Old City cobblestone streets downhill from me, near the Abuhav Shul. A direct hit into the Midreshet Tzafnat Women's Seminary. *Baruch Hashem*, no one was there.

I walked home quickly, for safety's sake and because I needed to talk to someone. I knew whom I would speak to first. When I arrived home, I opened my siddur to *minchah*.

Midreshet Tzafnat courtyard after the missile strike

"G-ttenyu," I began, because my mother always called Him G-ttenyu.

"What does 'G-ttenyu' mean?" I had asked my Rebbe many years ago. "Can I address Hashem this way?"

He had smiled. "It's a sweet term of endearment. Yes, you can."

"G-ttenyu," I said now, "thank You for protecting me. You never intended that missile to hurt me, I know that. But it wasn't just random chance that it exploded so close to my house. Why did You need to get my attention? What *teshuvah* am I ignoring that You want of me?"

I've stopped complaining that Hashem doesn't answer me. I have friends who get clear answers when they pray, like it's a two-way conversation. It's not like that for me. I've learned to pay attention to the first thought that comes to my mind after I've asked Him a question.

"Oh. Her. OK, I need to take care of that." I had offended a friend last week, and I hadn't made peace with her yet. "For such a little thing, You sent such a big boom?"

Hundreds, maybe thousands, of people had been terrified by that Katyusha blast ten minutes ago. I knew Our Creator had a reason for every single one of us.

"V'ahavta l'rei'acha kamocha, loving your fellow Jew like yourself, is no small thing. I know it's important, Hashem. But there must be something else. Please, tell me."

No answer. I finished davening.

A few hours later there were more sirens. More danger. I pushed my bed into the safe corner I had created in my bedroom, far from the windows. Sitting down on it, I propped my back up against the wall with pillows and got comfy in my "Katyusha corner." No booms. But you just never knew. They might still come.

Time for a cheshbon nefesh, a spiritual accounting. Chana, do you really believe that Hashem loves you? I asked myself. Or have you just been quoting the party line? How do you feel about Hashem now, after that Katyusha exploded so close to you today?

 formed formed formed

"Mommy, don't cry. Mommy, everything will be OK."

My mother wasn't the type to cry. Not since the Holocaust. But today she was crying. It was the worst day I could remember in my young life. Today was the day that we had to put the padlock on our little store and walk away. Nobody wanted it. My father would never get out of his job sewing in the uniform factory. And my mother would have to get a factory job now. They didn't let Jews go past the eighth grade in Poland. No education, no job.

"Mommy, everything will be OK! You'll see."

"After I'm dead, everything will be OK. You'll come to my grave, and you'll call down to me, 'Everything is good now.' For me, life will never be good."

So I learned young that Hashem didn't like us. Because if

Hashem didn't like my mother, then He didn't like me either. Other people He favored. But we weren't on that list. And there wasn't any way to get on that list.

That's what I thought for most of my life. Even though I grew up and prospered. And life really was good to me. *It's temporary. He's just giving me a little break before the next whack.*

The whacks came. And then I was more sure than when I was a child that my mother was right. It led to all those bad *middos* like selfishness, jealousy, and bitterness. I was sure of it when my mother passed away when I was twenty-one. And I was positive it was true when my father passed away some years later. My divorce cinched it.

Studying Torah let me see Hashem through new eyes. A whole lifetime had to be reframed. Hashem is all good and gives only good. It just doesn't look so good from our limited perspective in this finite world. I bought it. But I knew I only believed it in my head. My gut still believed that my mother was right. Chazal say that it is a forty-year journey from the head to the heart. And I haven't been religious yet for forty years. It's figurative anyway. Forty is symbolic of transformation. Before the Katyushas started exploding in July, I would have estimated that my belief in G-d's total goodness had worked its way down to about the middle of my neck.

Chana, does Hashem love you? I forced the question on myself. The explosion had blown away all the emotional and mental veils. My soul was a calm, clear sea. It was easier to see into myself than ever before. "Yes," I answered myself honestly. "Whether He chooses to end my life or make it more difficult with wounds or suffering, *chas v'shalom*, or whether He protects me from all harm, Hashem loves me. He loves me more than I will ever be able to comprehend while I am in this finite world. I'm sure. I believe it."

Wow. All the way from the brain to the heart and right on down into the kishkes.

So *teshuvah* can feel this way, too. No dramatics. No high. No tears. Just a good, deep, calm, honest answer.

I sighed. "Thank You, Hashem." Question and answer in less than two minutes.

cs cs cs

I left my Katyusha corner, walked into the living room, and flipped a few pages on the small weekly calendar hanging on the wall. Av was a heavy month for me for more reasons than Tishah B'Av. Two teachings of Chazal flashed in my mind in rhythm as I flipped the two calendar pages after Tishah B'Av.

Flip — I found my father's *yahrtzeit*, the sixteenth of Av. It is known that every year, on the *yahrtzeit*, each soul in Heaven is judged in order to ascend higher as it journeys ever closer to Hashem.

Flip — Here it is, my mother's *yahrtzeit*, six days after my father's, the twenty-second of Av. When a child does *teshuvah* over something negative he learned from a parent, the parent's soul is also rectified.

Mom, I finally learned in *Olam Hazeh* a smidgen of what you learned thirty-seven years ago when you entered the next world. Mom, get ready — you're really going up high this year!

Midreshet Tzafnat courtyard after the missile strike. Note the bookcase of untouched sefarim.

Day 5

Date: July 17, 2006 08:43:29 +0200
From: Johanna Yaffe
To: Tzefat under Fire list
Subject:

dear folks

Tzefat is closed down. a few food shops are open in the morning, and we are getting deliveries of the papers, bread, milk etc. the authorities patrol the streets in their cars, vans and what have you. a few people get off buses from out of town.

The mist hangs heavy over the hills, waiting for the sun to burn it off. It's more than usual — the smoke from the IDF's planes, artillery and so on has probably added to it. the spotter planes fly overhead from time to time, to check on forest fires, where Katyushas may have landed.

In the distance we hear booms from time to time — is it us or them? Who knows... Maybe we are hearing the echoes all the way from the IDF's barrage in Beirut, or maybe it's a bit closer to home. we stay in and do Sudoku, listen to the news endlessly, and play Freecell on the computer. there is the smell of cordite in the air. we could do with a good rainstorm to clear the air and change the energy. Sudden alarms of birds fly up into the sky, dogs bark in unison, and somewhere something lands, hopefully in open ground. we carry on in a lethargic, bored, end of the school summer holidays sort of way. We pray and give each other blessings and words of support, and talk to our friends on the telephone. we don't go

out. there are no cafes open for the ladies who lunch today.
take care
lots of love, johanna

• • •

From TzfatLine:

Item #4

MORE ADVICE:

The editors were advised by a friend in Tel Aviv that if you, or
your children, find shrapnel on the streets, DO NOT pick it up.
Chemicals may have been included in the "payload" and by
picking it up, you may be endangering yourself. Let it lie and let
it be swept up.

• • •

Date: July 17, 2006
From: Henry Klein
To: Chana Besser
Subject: Our prayers are with you always

Hi Ms. Besser,
Henry Klein here — your daughter Julie's friend from Colorado.
We're all glued to the news watching what's going on in Israel and
in Tzefat in particular. As someone who knows how frightening a
Katyusha rocket is, I am amazed by your courage and grace under
fire. All our prayers are with you in hopes of a quick ending to the
shelling and a quick return of Israeli soldiers home.
Keep your head down and stay safe! No heroics.
B'shalom, Henry

Date: July 17, 2006
From: Chana Besser
To: Henry Klein
Subject: Re: Our prayers are with you always

Hi Henry,

Thanks for writing!

How did you get experience with Katyushas?

Shabbos was good. Lots of Katyushas, but Hashem steered most of them where no one got hurt — mostly.

Have a good week, chana

Date: July 17, 2006
To: Chana Besser
From: Henry Klein
Subject: Re: Re: Our prayers are with you always

Hi Chana,

Glad the Katyushas are landing where you ain't! Stay low, let's pray this push will get rid of Hezbollah once and for all.

I grew up in Russia and saw the Katyusha rockets firsthand when I was in the Russian army. The ones I saw fired were from the newer arsenal, the 220 mm Uragan (Russian for Hurricane) and the even larger 300 mm Smerch (Tornado). None of these are in Lebanon (thank G-d) nor are they likely to make their way into the region. Both the Russians and the Chinese exported a bunch of the older, smaller models to both Syria and Iran in the 90s, some of which unfortunately (but not surprisingly) were smuggled into Lebanon.

All Katyushas are fired from trucks. The source of the launch is very easy to see at night due to the large amount of smoke and fire around the launch site, which makes them very visible to the planes above. That's why they are being launched only during the daylight.

Both the US and Israel have been working anti-Katyusha defense systems for the last decade. The early warning systems are already in place and the actual interception stations are soon to come online. The interception systems will also stop the Kassam rockets from the south, so both threats will soon become a thing of the past.

Take care and be safe, Henry

• • •

Agudath Israel of America calls on all Jews to respond to the alarming situation in Eretz Yisrael with intensified determination to merit Hashem's help for our brethren in the Holy Land.

Let us reinvigorate our tefillos and our recitation of Tehillim — especially kapitlach 83, 130, and 142 — each morning after davening, followed by the tefillah of "Acheinu Kol Beis Yisrael," as the Moetzes Gedolei HaTorah suggested five years ago. At that time, the Moetzes Gedolei HaTorah stressed as well that each Jewish man should be very careful regarding davening with a minyan, that all his tefillos, shacharis, minchah, and ma'ariv, be part of a "prayer of the multitude," which is always heard.

They emphasized as well that we should arrive early enough at shul to recite all of Pesukei D'Zimrah, and that righteous women, too, should undertake to say the above chapters of Tehillim in their homes each day and to set aside tzedakah for the poor of Eretz Yisrael.

In the merit of our prayers and our deeds, may we soon see the obliteration of evil in our world and the arrival of the go'el tzedek, quickly, in our days.

• • •

Date: July 17, 2006
From: Cheryl Mirrop
To: Chana Besser
Subject: Denver Rally

Dear Chana,
I've been getting my updates from Julie. Sounds like you are re-

maining very strong in the face of what has been happening. Just wanted to let you know that there was a "last-minute" Israel rally at BMH this past Sunday — it looked to me like there were nearly 2000 people there from everywhere in Denver. All kinds of rabbis were there... All kinds of Jews. Everyone was unified at that rally, and the feeling of so many kinds of Jews in one place was very strong. Everyone cried together, sang together, and prayed together. We were truly "one people," and I felt that we were sending the energy of unity to Israel. I pray that this energy from Denver reaches Israel so Israel can be unified where all Jews are one family.

Once we become one, our enemies will have no chance against us.

I'm saying tehillim for Israel every day.

Love, Cheryl

Date: July 17, 2006 13:25:35 EDT
From: Linda Green
To: Chana Besser
Subject: I'm Yiftach's mom

Dear Chana,

Yiftach, my son, sends me your letters daily. I can only say that my soul has awakened and you have made me so proud to be a Jew. Bless your courage.

I'm coming to Beit Shemesh and Jerusalem in two weeks and will lend any support I can to my children. If you need me, let me know.

Linda Green

Linda came to Israel, and found a family from the North to help during their wartime stay in Beit Shemesh. Way to go, Linda!

NOGA DOBKIN

Update

Tuesday, July 18, 2006
22 Tammuz 5766

I 'm taking a break from the bomb shelter to update you. How does one describe fear, or put into words the horrible sounds of nonstop missiles falling near my home? We are so close to the border that we hear the sirens a few seconds after the missiles land. When we hear a rocket striking, we wonder exactly where and what happened, *Hashem yishmor*.

Sometimes it's so close that our ears hurt from the blast, and we wonder if it hit our building. Did it fall next door? Was someone hurt, G-d forbid, or wounded, or did it fall between buildings? The sounds of our brave army boys flying overhead mix with the wails of frightened or hungry or just bored children.

So we sit in the shelter, at times gasping for lack of fresh air, waiting for a quiet fifteen minutes so we can open the door and stand outside a bit. The eerie sound of the whistling rocket flying overhead and landing with a heart-stopping thud and breaking out in fire. Oh, I forgot to describe the smell of the fire. It smells.

We live in the Canaan neighborhood of Tzefat. The bomb shelter in our building is shared by a family of fourteen, a family of twelve, a family of eight, two young couples, and our family of eight, including my mother-in-law, who has been with us throughout this war. There's a family of seven that doesn't come down to the shelter.

There is no bathroom, no running water, and only weak lightbulbs. Since we live closest to the shelter, everyone uses our bathroom. We brought in an extension cord from our house for a fan — it moves the stale air around some — and a night light. I am grateful that we can be of help.

I'm so proud of our girls. Our children are the oldest, so Rivka, Shaina, and Bracha are running a wonderful bomb shelter camp for all the younger kids until 2 p.m. every day. They keep the kids occupied and give the parents a needed break.

The children need to be kept busy, so we shlepped the owner of an arts-and-crafts store out of his shelter to buy crafts and games. We also help with getting all the kids bathed and tucked in. At night we spread out all the mattresses. In the morning, we stack them up to make room for the day's activities.

No one works now, so there's no income. Clothing is always scarce for these families. Now the even fewer changes of clothes are being ruined from the conditions of the shelter. We won't have many clothes left for the kids once we get out of here.

Obviously, there is no time to cook meals from scratch. Fast food costs a fortune in Israel. Mothers run up to their third- or fourth-floor apartments from our basement bomb shelter, heat up some food in the microwave, and run down to their children, afraid to be left alone during an attack. To me, the frightening sounds of the missiles falling are less horrible than the sounds of the children (from babies to nineteen years old) screaming and crying during an attack. "Mommy! Mommy! Where's Mommy? Did the missile get her?"

Pray for us. Those of you who are calling me all the time to find out how we are and saying that you wished you could help in some way, please, say *tehillim* for all of Israel and for us.

Day 6

Date: July 18, 2006 23:09:41 +0200
From: Chana Besser
To: Tzefat under Fire list
Subject: The 3 hurt today in Tzefat are going to be OK

The 7 p.m. news in Israel said that 52 or 53 missiles were fired on Tzefat today. They fired over 80 missiles on the whole North. (Sorry, I don't know the exact numbers for the gematria buffs.) One person was killed in Nahariya, baruch Dayan ha'emes, six wounded in Haifa.

They reported three people injured in Tzefat and five treated for shock. I called a man in Hatzalah and he says they are all going to be OK, none of them seriously hurt. He said, "Big miracles — miracles everywhere, all the time." He didn't have a second more to talk to me.

Today's target in Tzefat was the Industrial District in the extreme south of town, below the Tzefat cemetery. The hospital is near the industrial district and so is the large community of Me'or Chaim. Rivka says there are just nine families left in her building today, 10% of the residents. I'm not going out to conduct a census, but that feels about right to me for the Old City, too.

• • •

The first 100 families in Tzefat who are out of grocery money and call Noson Rosenberg, courtesy of Eizer L'Shabbos, will get grocery deliveries in time to cook for Shabbos. He can be reached starting Wednesday morning at his grocery store in Me'or Chaim.

• • •

Hafrashas challah this Thursday throughout Israel

This Thursday at 6 p.m. all women in Israel are invited to do hafrashas challah with a berachah. Hope you have enough flour. That's a good time when people in other time zones could join if you wish. If anyone is wondering what that is, consult your nearest Orthodox rabbi or religious woman.

• • •

Call 106 for information daily on what is open and when. They said that one bank was open today, didn't know which one. Two or more banks will be open tomorrow. Today Supersol and Hypernetto supermarkets were open. The independents are mostly open, but 106 doesn't seem to know about them.

• • •

Date: July 18, 2006
From: Chana Besser
To: Tzefat under Fire list
Subject: The chickens are starving

My landlord's son, Yochai Trabelsi, asked me to feed his chickens. They ate well on Shabbos scraps, but now I have nothing to feed them. If you live close by or have to be on my street anyway, please — would you save your food garbage? They tell me the chickens eat everything, but they walked away from all the potato and carrot peels I gave them this morning, and I only peeled them for the chickens.

Please, help! One who shows rachamim for animals, Hashem will show rachamim for them.

I bless you for safety, with all of klal Yisrael.

chana

CHANA BESSER

Chickens

"Chickens who don't eat potato peels are not hungry."
Sarah Kopp wrote to me. "They can exist on stale
bread that people leave on the garbage cans."

In the middle of a war, I'm dashing to neighbors. For chickens. I ring the chief rabbi's doorbell.

"Rebbetzin, I have the smallest problem of this war. Would that all our problems be so small."

I am probably the only person in Tzefat to call Tova Eliyahu "rebbetzin." Everyone else calls her "rabbanit" — the Sefardic pronunciation. But I know that she's a Polish girl. The first time I called her "rebbetzin" she smiled from ear to ear. Now she only smiles inside. When I first came here in 1995, I didn't speak Hebrew. We used to speak Yiddish back then. Don't tell anyone she knows Yiddish. They won't believe you anyway. Her father-in-law is Rav Mordechai Eliyahu, the former chief rabbi of Israel. He wears a tall turban and royal robes, Sefardi-style.

The "rebbetzin" promised to collect her leftovers for the chickens and gave me lots of stale bread.

"Moisten it with water. They like it that way."

Chaya came with some soup veggies. The chickens loved her food. Chaya graduated from vet school.

"They're not eating much, and they're not laying eggs," I told her.

"They're probably scared by the sirens and the Katyushas. Just keep giving them clean water, clean out their feeding trough, and put out new food every day. If they are hungry, they will eat."

Several days later, when I had nothing left for them, I dashed back to the chief rabbi's house. She hadn't forgotten. The *rebbetzin* pulled two big plastic boxes out of her fridge, each one the size of a shoe box.

"Cholent. From Shabbat."

"Great. The chickens are getting *sherayim*!"

I'd rather stay at my computer, but nobody else is going to feed the chickens.

ADINAH ROSEN

Choose Life

Thursday, July 20, 2006
24 Tammuz 5766

Miraculous days bring clearer insights. After Tuesday's fifty-two rockets shot at Tzefat and only three people lightly injured, *baruch Hashem*, I woke up Wednesday morning with an insight that was to me the kernel of this war.

There are four holy cities in the Land of Israel, and each is connected to an element. Chevron is earth, since the Patriarchs and Matriarchs — Sarah and Avraham, Rivka and Yitzchak, Leah and Yaakov — are buried there. Jerusalem is fire, since it is the heart where the eternal flame burns and where the Temple once stood with its offerings. Tiberias is water, since the main body of inland water is there. And Tzefat is air, the mystical city.

Someone asked a holy man the other day, "Why is Tzefat being so heavily bombarded?"

He said: "Because Tzefat is a holy city, and the source of evil behind this is the head of Iran. The source of evil is trying to destroy holiness."

This gave a new meaning to the endless boom, boom, booming, and made it a little easier to hear. But holiness, evil...what does that really mean?

Wednesday morning it came to me.

Tzefat is the city of air and air is life. Life itself is equated with holiness. "The holiness of life," the teachings say.

The tzaddik of Tzefat, the holy Ari, *z"l*, who brought Kabbalah into the form that we know it today, teaches that all the faces of Creation are also within each individual.

"Adam is a small universe. The universe is a large Adam."

I always love looking at this passage hanging up in the square of the Old City near the health food store. Hmmmm... So somehow this war outside, all the rockets landing in Tzefat, reflects something going on within me and everyone else on the planet. An inner war within all individuals playing itself out in Technicolor where the players are Israel and entities within the Muslim world.

This is the war between choosing life and choosing death. Terrorists blow themselves up, send children out to the front line, and hide behind innocent people in their fight to bring death to others. And then they glorify it. This is the most extreme expression of choosing death.

We all have a bit of this dark force within us. Death is the lack of life force within something. Lack, our sense of lack that eats at our innards, is an expression of feeling dead within. When we are hungry, our body is saying, "I am in the process of decay, and if some life force — food — is not provided, I will die." We have no choice in this most basic aspect of lack within ourselves. We must choose life.

But there are the other lacks that are within our realm of choosing life or choosing death.

Appreciation is an active expression of choosing life, as opposed to focusing on the lack. Articulating conscious appreciation for even the littlest things brings more of a sense of life. Try a day of consciously appreciating everything, even the water coming out of the tap. Ahhh...life.

Believing in oneself is an expression of choosing life. The more I believe in my ability to become who I was truly created to be, that I have a purpose, the more life comes through me. Fear comes from not humbly believing that becoming one's unique self is a unique gift to the planet, that there is a purpose to one's existence.

Fear is intertwined with focusing on the lack. We all know how fear literally creates a feeling of tightness, shortness of breath, blockage, disconnection — expressions of death. Hearing the *boom boom* outside, I watch these Technicolor vibrations of death, intended to bring fear and destruction, trying to shake me from remembering that there is purpose and that who I truly am can never be wiped out.

This ignites another thought to contemplate in this hologram of "everything that is happening in the physical world represents inner dimensions that are within us all."

What is this "desire for death" hiding deeply, intertwined within our desire for life? Perhaps if we all contemplate and find it within ourselves, we can help protect these innocent people who are being used as shields for the death focus and the soldiers who are having to directly interact with it. Where do we try to fool ourselves, make justifications or blame others, because of our lack of appreciation and lack of belief in who we uniquely are? Low self-esteem combined with not appreciating what one has, whether it be physical or spiritual accomplishments on any level, will inevitably lead to blame and putting others down. In a sense, it's "killing" another person in order to lift ourselves up and out of the sense of lack.

And still another thought arises. In Israel now (and outside) there is a tremendous sense of coming together, a sense of love and care. Even in the economic arena. The hotels in Jerusalem are giving discounts for citizens in the north. There is free entrance to the zoo, discounts at grocery stores... But why do we need to have our existence threatened in order to come to a place of unity, cooperation, deep caring? This is something to think about when we are searching for the phenomena within ourselves. Everything that is happening on the outside collectively is happening within us individually.

ADINAH ROSEN teaches chassidic thought at the Sha'arei Binah Seminary for Women in Tzefat. She is involved in international intercultural work and local environmental programs.

Day 8

Date: July 20, 2006
From: Hannah Levi
To: Chana Besser
Subject: Baruch Hashem

The day before the war started, my two girls were going to day camp with their school in Tzefat. At 8:00 a.m. they went to their school and the teacher was preparing them for their trip.

An argument broke out between two of the girls. One of them ran away and could not be found anywhere. The teacher said they were not going on the tiyul till the girl came back, so they searched and waited. About 10 a.m. the girl was found and brought back to the group. The girls were disappointed that the trip was leaving so late. They left on the bus two hours later than planned.

Meanwhile, a Katyusha rocket hit the park that they would have been at had they left on time!

And my younger girls are usually in gan until 3:30 p.m., but on the first day of bombing in Tzefat (Thursday), because it was a fast day (17 Tammuz) they came home at 12 p.m. One of the first rockets fell on the Mazuda (Fortress) right next to their gan at 2.45 p.m.! Baruch Hashem, nobody was there.

Date: July 20, 2006
From: Chana Besser
To: Tzefat under Fire list
Subject: 13-year-old: "I want to stay, Rebbetzin!"

Rebbetzin Sheinberger gets many calls for advice, but not usually from 13-year-olds. "Rebbetzin, do I have to leave Israel? I want to stay. I totally understand why my father told me I couldn't go home to Tzefat the first day of the shelling. I was in Jerusalem in a summer camp, and he wouldn't let me go back. I listened to him, even though I wanted to be in Tzefat. He's my father, and of course I have to honor him. So I've been staying in Jerusalem. I miss my mother and little sister. They're at home in Tzefat.

"That was bad enough, but now my grandparents insist that our whole family has to leave Israel until the war is over, and none of us want to go. They have been pressuring my mother every day for weeks, and they are pretty hysterical by now. My mother decided that she has to honor her parents, no matter how much she hates going to America. She totally doesn't fit in there. I mean, can you see her at the country club?

"Isn't it forbidden to leave Eretz Yisrael when the Holy Land is under siege? I want to go back to Tzefat. I don't want to abandon Eretz HaKodesh like this. It's bad enough being away from my town when she needs me. But do we have to go all the way to America?"

A very unhappy family boarded the airplane, but not until they had bought a set of Tehillim divided into twenty pamphlets to distribute on the flight.

RIFCA GOLDBERG

War Diary

This is Rifca Goldberg's Tzefat war diary. She lives in the Me'or Chaim neighborhood, about a fifteen-minute walk from the center of town. It consists of four huge apartment buildings, each thirteen stories high with three entrances. Approximately ninety apartments are in each complex, two to four apartments per floor.

Me'or Chaim, Tzefat
Thursday, July 13 (17 Tammuz)

Today I told a woman from Australia not to be afraid after this morning's bombings. I told her that I've lived in Safed nearly two decades, and there have never been any wars in Safed. Safed is the safest place in the world.

Later in the day I went to buy vegetables in a store on the main street of Safed. As I was paying, there was a huge boom. The store shook, the glass shattered above us, and I started screaming. I covered my mouth with my hand to stop myself since there were two children in the store and I didn't want to frighten them more than they were already frightened. I finished paying with shaking hands and walked home as quickly as I could. People in the street were crying from fear. As I came down the hill, I could see Mount Meron smoking and I could hear sirens wailing.

Friday, July 14 (18 Tammuz)

I woke up today to the sounds of bombing and helicopters whirling above — at least the latter are on our side!

It's weird how little the news is reporting. People are spending hours in the bomb shelters, but I can't since I'm asthmatic and the closed-in, airless, dusty bomb shelter is more of a threat for me than being in my house. Anyway, I don't believe it'll go on too long.

Those of us who are still here, staying for Shabbos, are somewhat calmer than those evacuating, so at least the panic level is not so intense. Meanwhile, here in Safed the rumors are flying faster and harder than the missiles! I won't believe anything until I hear it from a reliable source.

I have to get ready for Shabbos. It's a weird feeling having to ask oneself, "Should I risk my life by going to the mini-market and buying challos, or should I send my twenty-year-old son and, G-d forbid, risk his life?"

So many people are leaving for Shabbos, but I'm sure Shabbos will be quiet. I'm sure of it.

Motza'ei Shabbos, July 15 (19 Tammuz)

Shabbos was like a thunderstorm. The entire day and all night was nonstop — literally nonstop — bombing, jets, helicopters, ambulances. Whenever the kids squabbled I would say, "There's a war outside! We don't need one inside, too!" They settled down quickly. The constant noise of bombing outside said more than I could.

Two of my boys came home after davening and told me about a Katyusha shell that fell about a block and a half from our apartment. It fell on the side of a hill with no homes and no people. "It was about six feet long and thin. We watched it hit, explode, and burst into flames. Ima, it was beautiful! Like the Lag Ba'Omer fire, only bigger."

I had no response. I would never think of a bomb as "beautiful," but that's the perspective of a child. They see things so differently.

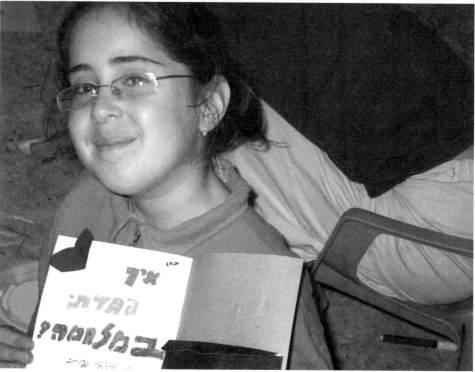

Keeping the kids busy in the bomb shelters

According to my count, the Safed area has had over 300 hits in three days, but it's probably more. It just doesn't stop. Three were within a couple blocks of my house, rocking the whole building complex!

I wish I could write something good, but right now I can't. I keep praying, telling the kids stories of all the times we've come out victorious against all odds. It's so scary. My stomach is in constant knots; the kids are all clingy.

A lot of people are frantic to leave Safed. I guess I wasn't the only one who thought that Shabbos would be quiet. The bus stops are filled, the buses overflowing.

Sunday, July 16 (20 Tammuz)

I'm not just receiving e-mails, but also e-hugs, e-kisses, e-love, and e-prayers! Everyone cares so much. I wish we felt more united without having to go through these kinds of trials and tribulations.

My sixteen-year-old waited to catch the bus back to Bnei Brak, but it was so full that the driver wouldn't let him on and he had to wait for the next one. That one was also too full, but the driver allowed him to sit on the steps.

Since the evening, the bombs have been falling fast and furious, sirens wailing in the blackness of the night. I can't sleep.

Monday, July 17 (21 Tammuz)

I went to the mini-market to do the weekly shopping. I'm afraid to go out of the house, but we do need food! Inside the store there was only one other woman and the cashier. "How am I going to get through all these crowds of people to do my shopping?" I joked.

She chuckled and said, "Yeah, the whole three families that are left in Safed. It certainly has emptied out. This time of year Safed is usually packed with tourists and guests. Not now. It feels more like a ghost town."

There were only three men in my husband's shul today. He'll have to try to find a minyan in a different shul. Other families have left or people are too nervous to leave the bomb shelters. But where can he find a minyan in our neighborhood? Everything's closed down — no school, no intercity buses, no stores other than the grocery stores, which are open for a couple of hours a day (or "until a bomb falls," they tell me when I call), and my husband has to go into work at the pharmacy for a few hours a day. It's termed "emergency procedure." This is the second war I've been in (the first was the Gulf War), but it was never so close to home.

At the moment, we're doing fine, thank G-d. The truth is, today was much quieter up here. I think they decided that they did enough damage to Safed, although, as I write this, I hear bombs falling. Maybe it's in the surrounding areas, maybe the other side of Safed. I don't know. They're hitting Arab villages as well. They really don't care as long as they can do damage. We'll get through this, though — we Jews always have, always will.

Tuesday, July 18 (22 Tammuz)

A group of volunteers came to the bomb shelter. After two hours of games and singing and arts and crafts, the kids came home smiling and happy — they had a blast! (Maybe I shouldn't use that word...)

It's really boring being in the house 24/7, although today we had a bit of excitement. We watched eight missiles fall in the wadi below us, about two miles from us. They started fires, then these little planes flew out and poured red stuff over them to snuff them out.

Boy, are those Katyushas loud! At least the missiles that fall in the fields and valleys don't do so much damage. Of course, people's incomes are being seriously damaged due to hardly anyone working. I won't say anything about the damage from direct hits and the many, many wounded. The news is covering that and it hurts too much to write about it.

Even though we, personally, are doing OK, thank G-d, it's still tough. I don't pretend it's not.

Someone called today. Arrangements have been made for free transportation to Bnei Brak and free camps for a week or longer.

My boys don't want to go.

"They're not saying when we can come home," my twelve-year-old son said.

"I know, sweetheart, but they don't know for how long."

"Then I don't want to go," he said, his large hazel eyes wide with...fear? the unknown? wanting to be near me but not wanting to admit it?

How is one supposed to know what's best for one's children and family in a situation like this? Who says that one place is safer than another right now? Some of these decisions could be life-and-death decisions!

I close my eyes, inhale fully, and try to feel what's deep within me. In truth, I don't want the family to be separated. I don't want my children to go away. They'll stay. I let my breath out slowly. We'll be together and Hashem will be together with us, too.

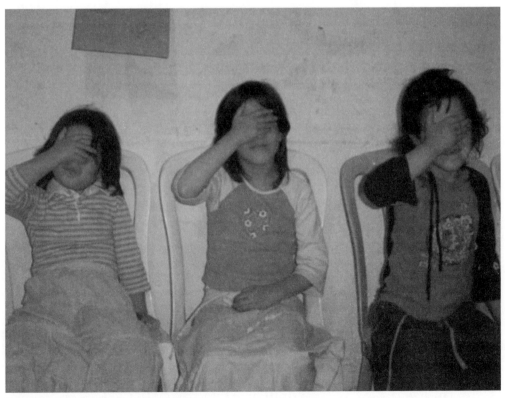

Reciting the morning Shema in a bomb shelter

Wednesday, July 19 (23 Tammuz)

This morning, my twelve-year-old went outside to "build." I don't usually yell at my kids but I certainly broke that pattern now. I yelled at him like I can't remember ever yelling at him. "NOT ONE TOE IS TO GO OUT OF THIS HOUSE!"

I told him I'll send him to Bnei Brak since he doesn't realize that there's a war going on. He's been good the whole day, poor kid. We've all been holed up for seven straight days now. How much can they play with Lego and read the same books over and over again? There are almost no neighbors left, and no one wants their kids out of their sight, so it's us, here, and that's it.

Thursday, July 20 (24 Tammuz)

Yated came out today and the poem I wrote last week was in it. My friend sent me this e-mail:

" 'Storming in the Holy Land' is amazing. No rhythm, which in this case really fits. It touches feelings that I buried long ago and am not sure I can find.

"I'm quietly going nuts, being away from my home in Safed. I miss having my own space, my own bed to sleep in, my own fridge and chair and everything! No rhythm to my life right now. This is the hardest part for me. I discover that my life is built on structures that are there to keep me safe — and some are hollow.

"Hang in. I don't know which is harder — having the bombs or being completely out of place. My son came with his wife so we are four families in a three-room flat. We've mostly been pay-ing for food, and it's been running close to 200 shekels a day. People who are nervous eat lots. And it's the only thing that will keep nerves down. Mine, anyway.

"I hold you safe in a huge huggggggggg."

She has a good point: at least I am in my own home with my own things. Having to go away might be quieter, it may be less dangerous, not as life-threatening, but it's not necessarily easier. So I do appreciate my friend's feelings of missing being in her home. I wish that she and every other "exile" could come home already. Soon. I really think it'll be soon.

The first several times that there were rounds of fifteen, twenty, or more bombings in quick succession, I called friends in Jerusalem or Bnei Brak just to get that link to normalcy, but they would have to get off the phone to take their kids to school or go to work.

I felt shocked: school? work? Such things exist right now? My life consists of *boom, boom,* and *boom!* To think that a two-and-a-half-hour drive away there is no war.

This afternoon was much quieter. There are I don't know how many bombings per minute, but now we're the ones shooting. Still, the noise...

I fall asleep around six o'clock in the afternoon and am awakened half an hour later by a siren near the house. All three boys fell asleep, too. This war is exhausting.

"Devory," I say to my youngest daughter, "you wake up Yitzchak Shneur, and I'll wake up the other two boys. They have to eat dinner and go to shul."

From Yitzchak Shneur's room I hear her singing out dramatically, "Yitzchak! Wake up! The *geulah* has arrived!"

I can't help but laugh.

My husband takes the boys to daven, but he's getting more and more concerned about having a minyan on Shabbos. The few people who are left seem to be leaving.

Meanwhile, a friend of mine is aching to come home and she calls me three times a day to find out exactly what's happening. Today is the first day that's quiet enough (or, at least, we're not the ones getting hit — "only" two hits in Safed that I know of...) that I tell her that considering where her apartment is located and because she doesn't have little children that, yes, now I'm finally willing to say that maybe it's OK for her to come back (until now I kept saying, "Not yet, not yet...").

"But I take no responsibility for the bus ride up here and take into account, my dear friend, the constant sounds of bombing and jets. It's very hard on the nervous system. Think it through carefully... Do you think you and your husband will be able to tolerate it?"

I can hear her thinking hard over the telephone line.

This is such a tense time. No one can make judgments on anyone. Every person, couple, and family has so many angles to consider. Everyone has to do what's right for himself.

Friday, July 21 (25 Tammuz)

I woke up at 3:00 a.m. I lay in bed for a full hour and a half listening to the jets soaring through the sky. I hoped for a five-minute interval so that I might be able to fall asleep again, but there wasn't even a one-minute interval. I wonder if my friends who call think I'm exaggerating when I say it's nonstop bomb-ing. I wish it were exaggeration...

At 4:30 a.m., I decided to get up. After sitting and writing for a while, I turn to look out the window at the olive tree swaying gen-tly in the breeze outside my apartment and there are birds hopping from branch to branch. The sun is rising, and it dawns on me that I haven't seen any animals for the past nine days! I take out the garbage and see something I haven't seen in over a week: cats. Two of them pawing their way through the bags and scraps of food. The animals have been holed up the same as we've been!

But now they're back. We can all hear the bombing still go-ing on in Lebanon, but the birds and the cats are coming back. G-d willing, the residents of Safed will start wending their way back to the dawn of normal life.

As I get my candles ready for Shabbos, all I can think, hope, and pray for is when the day will arrive when "the Merciful One will let us inherit that day which will be all Shabbos...for life ev-erlasting."

Amen!

RIFCA GOLDBERG is a mother of seven and grandmother of two. Her family has been living in Tzefat for over two decades. One of her favorite things to do in life is to write. Her writings have been in *Yated Ne'eman, Hamodia, Soferet, The Jewish Observer*, and the anthologies *Heartbeats* and *Salt, Pepper & Eternity*.

Day 9

Date: July 21, 2006
From: Chana Besser
To: Tzefat under Fire list
Subject: Early afternoon erev Shabbos

I wish I could tell you that the quiet we've been enjoying for the past few days — more or less — is continuing. By quiet I mean only five or six explosions outside town this morning, far enough away to walk freely outdoors. But it didn't last. We are a prime target again, starting early this afternoon. They waited until these afternoon hours erev Shabbos to launch a hard hit on Tzefat. They know we are getting ready for Shabbos now.

Friends called me from their refugee apartment in Ramat Beit Shemesh (outside Jerusalem) shortly after the explosions in Tzefat earlier today. They already knew where the missiles had fallen in Tzefat. Their friend had just seen three missiles go zooming right over his head in the Artists' Quarter and called them right away. I'm just four or five blocks from there. At least four loud blasts rattled my windows in the Old City — no more than they rattle from an overhead sonic boom. I don't know where the missiles landed, and I don't know if anyone was hurt, G-d forbid.

That's one of the worst things about the war for those of us in the North. After we hear the explosions, we don't know what happened. They don't want to broadcast too much detail because of enemy intelligence. (Anyone dumb enough to attack Hashem's chosen people make the expression "enemy intelligence" an oxymoron!) By the time the relatives are notified, it's a new day and the media has forgotten about yesterday's news. Meanwhile, we wonder and exchange rumors. Most of the civilians treated are well enough to walk into the hospital, and they go straight home after outpatient treatment for shock and shrapnel. Even those seriously injured mostly seem to be released from the hospital and have excellent chances of a full recovery. We are still very worried about a family with two children in serious condition.

A lady lives on the top of the bridge in the center of town, across from the Cave of Shem and Ever. She was very close to a few of those blasts today, and by 2 p.m. she was on the last erev Shabbos bus out of town. She said the bus was packed, so she's not the only one who left in a hurry. I guess they feared a repeat of last Shabbos.

"Hey, lady! Geveret!"

"Me?"

Two guys were standing outside my living room window, their arms filled with parcels of food.

"They're giving out food at the Soup Kitchen. They have cholent, soup, chicken, salads, all kinds of Shabbos food. Go and get whatever you need!"

"Thanks. Baruch Hashem, I don't need."

I've been in Israel long enough now. It's perfectly acceptable in Hebrew grammar to end a sentence with words like need, let, and want. We boldly let it invade our English sentence structure.

Amazing what spiritually and emotionally fragile creatures we are. My "oh so secure, I'm getting used to this and it's not so bad" confidence of the last few days shattered in a millisecond with that two-blocker. "Abba!" I had screamed to my Creator and Sustainer. Interesting, Chana. In a moment of fear, you called Hashem Abba, I said to myself. Why did you do that? My father was Tatte when I was little. Then he became Daddy. He was never Abba. Congratulations, you just took another small step towards becoming an Israeli.

I have to do a little cleaning now. It's only in honor of Shabbos, because I assure you, I'm not going to have any guests. Bless us, and I want to bless you, too, with a Shabbat Shalom.

git Shabbos,

chana

• • •

July 21, 2006

For Tzefat, Cooked Mehadrin Meals

Available Friday morning 9:30 until supplies run out.

800 Cooked mehadrin carry-out food portions provided by fund-raising by Rabbi Simcha and Elisheva Mirvis for Eizer L'Shabbos.

Shnitzel, veggies, rice — a full balanced meal.

First come, first serve.

Me'or Chaim Grocery Store (bottom of Building 4).

Call for delivery to distant neighborhoods.

CHANA BESSER

The Second Shabbos under Fire

Shabbos, July 22, 2006
26 Tammuz 5766

Two Friday afternoons in a row without my landlady's couscous. It's a high price to pay for enduring a war. "Hi, Mom! This is an excellent time to come see me in America!"

I listened to the telephone message from Cindy, my younger daughter, just before candle-lighting time. *She doesn't understand. She parachutes out of helicopters to ski ungroomed slopes, and she thinks I'm being reckless?* Becoming religious later in life presents family challenges during the best of times.

Shabbos in Tzefat came in with lots of Katyushas booming throughout the afternoon, but not as close to my neighborhood as our first Shabbos under fire. We were war-wise veterans by now. It took more to shake us. I accepted invitations within a block for both Shabbos meals and didn't cook anything. I wasn't as afraid to stay home as I had been last week. Now we knew how long to wait after the last boom before it was safe to dash out.

"Hashem, I could really use a Carlebach minyan," I whispered as I finished my davening alone again this Shabbos. The Beirav

Shul was closed. Its roof was flat and weak and would not hold out in the face of a rocket attack.

I heard strong, joyful singing. "It's coming from Kikar Maginim!"

I quickened my steps. It was hard to believe my eyes. Rav Shmuel Eliyahu, the chief rabbi of Tzefat, and a group of about twenty men were singing and dancing in the square, under the temporarily quiet starry sky — a Carlebach *Kabbalas Shabbos*.

I joined the small group of women, teenage girls, and little children standing off to the side, near the snack kiosk. One *niggun* blended into another and another and another. I walked down the street, skipping in my heart, not wanting to leave.

Rachel's surprised pleasure alerted me. I had confused my two invitations.

"I was supposed to come for lunch, wasn't I?"

"Yes, but I invited you for both meals."

"The Meyers will worry if I don't come, and their children will be disappointed. They always have so many guests, and they haven't had a guest since the war began. Here, these grapes are for you for Shabbos. I'll see you tomorrow." A kiss and I was off, leaving my confused friend behind.

It's war stress, Chana, I admitted to myself. *How many times have you gone to the wrong house for a Shabbos meal before? Zero.* I got to walk through the square again. The number of people had doubled. Breslov chassidim on their way home after *tefillah* had joined. The women's section had doubled, too.

"That rabbi over there flew in from Riverdale, New York, to be in Tzefat this Shabbos," whispered Miriam. A Jerusalem family and an American *yeshivah bachur* learning in Jerusalem were here, too. The *chizuk* was working. Everyone had big smiles. Hearts were light for the first time. And the skies were quiet — for now.

The men sang more. The joy grew. And grew. And grew. "Now we are making Hashem happy." Avital Shira grabbed my hand, her face glowing. This was the first time I had seen her smile since she had come back from Amona. *The more we have suffered, the more we will rejoice,* I thought.

 times times times

The Meyer children were very happy to see me. Most of their building was empty. They didn't even care about the brown sugar and honey lollipops I had brought, usually the focus of the younger girls' attention. I was right. It was very good for them to have a guest. *Chizuk*.

"The chickens are eating, by the way."

Chaya had brought me food scraps and given me advice on taking care of them.

"The sirens go off so often without any shelling," I added.

"That's because the missiles launched over Tzefat could come down in Tiveria or Chatzor, or any other northern town, *chas v'shalom*, and we would never hear them," the older Meyer girls educated me. "The sirens are set off by electronic sensors." It didn't surprise me that they knew about the technology of sirens and missiles.

times times times

"Ima, come back!" the children screamed, terrified. The night air was still. Chaya had stepped outside to escort me a few feet as I left for home.

"Go back. It's too frightening for them. I'll take a raincheck on the mitzvah of escorting out a guest."

times times times

Morning. Two of the three chubby Shabbos candle glasses were broken, and all three were scorched black. I like to pour oil into the glass, almost to the top of the candle, so that they burn all night. I love to come home Shabbos night after the meal to the soft glow of candlelight. This Shabbos most of the lights were on without a timer, even my bedroom, just in case. There was no oil spilled. A Katyusha boom must have shattered them after dawn.

"Come early for Shabbos lunch," Rachel had told me. "They always shell when they know people are walking to and from shul. I'll bet you never ate a Shabbos *seudah* in a clothing *gemach* before," she added with a laugh. It was safer than their home nearby.

Don't look at that beautiful fabric. You'll want to know if it fits you, I told myself. *And don't look there or there or there.* I couldn't find a place to rest my eyes. The clothing on the racks almost brushed up against our table and chairs on three sides. I love clothes. I love fabrics and textures and colors. *Chana, it's two aveiros on Shabbos — wanting something you don't have and planning. Look somewhere else.*

I focused on a collection of porcelain dolls. I don't want porcelain dolls.

Rachel's husband, Moshe, was giving a thought-provoking *devar Torah* when a Katyusha struck close by. It wasn't close enough to shake the walls or break the windows.

"I hear ambulance sirens."

"I don't."

"They are pretty far away."

We went back to the *devar Torah*.

"Sorry the nuts are so coarse. The air raid siren went off Friday while I was chopping them," Elisheva, another guest, explained as we ate her cake.

I heard *shalosh seudos zemiros* while I was having my third meal alone with my favorite *sefer, Tiferes Shlomo*. It sounded like thirty or forty men singing. It was coming from the Sanz Shul. Later, on my way to the Meyers for Havdalah, I saw half the men inside were wearing white and half were wearing black. That's more diversity than normal for Tzefat. Each of the Meyers' children recited "G-tt fun Avraham" three times. The children are always soothed by reciting *tehillim* and holy words. I've noticed this with all of my friends' children since the Katyushas began. While they are concentrating and reciting, a peaceful look comes over their faces.

I fell asleep that night praying for true peace, but knowing that very likely we would still be at war next Shabbos, too.

Parts of this essay were first published in *Hamodia* weekly newspaper.

Day 10

Date: July 22, 2006
From: Chana Besser
To: Tzefat under Fire list
Subject: Shavua tov, I'm alive and well

Lots of booms over Shabbos, but long intervals of quiet between them. All the shelling was concentrated around the times when the men walk to and from shul, the Shabbos seudos, and ma'ariv. May Hashem protect us all for the coming week, the coming month, the coming year.

Shavua tov,

Chana

Day 11

Date: July 23, 2006
From: Chana Besser
To: Tzefat under Fire list
Subject: Check this out

Gotta share this e-mail exchange with everyone. Our friend, Yehudit (see her e-mail below), is seventy-three years old, and she's running around, driving her car to help out people in the middle of these missile attacks. Yehudit was in America and returned to Tzefat the first week of the war, just like her airline ticket had been booked. Welcome home, Yehudit!

I love you!!!

From: Yehudit
To: Chana Besser
Subject: Sure I came home, right on schedule

I was visiting my children and grandchildren in California and Oregon when the war started. Five days later, at the end of my trip, family and friends protested that I stay on. I felt compelled to return to Tzefat and be of whatever value that I could. I well remember our Jews facing it alone during World War II. I couldn't live with myself if I were to take refuge in the USA while my people were under siege.

Some friends and I went out every day to visit soldiers in the Sieff

Hospital and the bomb shelters. I figured that since there are very few cars available, my car was needed to help out, and maybe the Big One will protect me if only for that.

We brought the soldiers candy, Tehillim, and words of Torah and offered them a letter written for them in a sefer Torah, which the Lubavitcher Rebbe said is powerful for protection and love for all Jews in an eternal common bond. Their gratefulness was unbound-ed.

One soldier, who had come out of surgery a few hours before, cried and said that he couldn't believe that religious women would even speak to a nonreligious soldier, as he referred to himself. I told him that we are all Jews, that we all love one another, that Hashem loves each and every one of us, and that His love and devotion to our holy land is a manifestation of the highest form of Torah-con-nection. He couldn't believe that I would say such a thing. He cried even more, and blessed each of us. We visited during sirens and sometimes took shelter. After a while, we just stopped thinking and asked Hashem to do our work with us.

• • •

From Sunday's TzfatLine:

Item #7

INVITATION:

Ann in Jerusalem telephone 02 _____ has room for two adults and three children, more if necessary, and they don't mind squashing up and using mattresses. They are child-friendly and have cribs, high chairs, strollers toys, and games and don't mind noise and mess! Food is included. For as long as is necessary.

Item #9

ENGLISH LIBRARY OPEN:

Edyth wants everyone to know that those wishing to avail them-selves of the books and other materials in the library may come any time during the day. If you don't want to borrow anything, you are welcome to just come and chat.

Item #10

HEALTH FOOD DELIVERY AVAILABLE:

Moshe Friedman of Teva Center in Kiryat Chabad will take telephone orders for health foods, vitamins, etc. 052-_____.
He will deliver to your door.

• • •

Date: July 23, 2006
From: Chana Besser
To: Avi
Subject: Looting

> At 12:38 23/07/2006, you wrote:
> Chana,
> What is the situation with theft and looting?
> I want to come up and check my daughter's apartment.
> Thanks,
> Avi

To date, I haven't heard of any looting in Tzefat. If you were a thief, G-d forbid, would you choose Tzefat? That would take some special kind of dumb. Every town has more to steal than Tzefat. I mean, half the houses don't have TV sets or computers. Now, if you are talking about the wealth of Torah, Tzefat is right up there at the top of the list.
Call Yehudit. I'm sure she'll go and check the apartment for you.
chana

Date: July 23, 2006
From: Chana Besser
To: Tzefat under Fire list
Subject: Tiferes Shlomo on why Israel is under attack

To understand the deepest, deepest reason, the penimiyus most inside reason, for our suffering, and what we have to do to keep our Holy Land, here is a very deep, deep Torah by the Tiferes Shlomo (the Radomsker Rebbe, Rav Shlomo HaKohen Rabinowitz, zt"l), translated by Avraham Sutton:

The daughters of Tzelafchad have a just claim.

(Bemidbar 27:7)

The tribe of Yosef's descendants have a just claim.

(Bemidbar 36:6)

Why, in these two verses, does the Torah repeat itself, saying [first], "The daughters of Tzelafchad have a *just claim*," and then, "The tribe of Yosef's descendants have a *just claim*"? Why wasn't this mitzvah given to them in the same manner as all of the mitzvos of the Torah? Also, why is it necessary to say afterward, "They may marry anyone who is good in their eyes" (*Bemidbar 36:6*)? Certainly they would not take someone [for a husband] who was not "good in their eyes."

It seems to me that this is the proper understanding of this matter: Behold, it is known that Yosef HaTzaddik embodies the *yesod dikedushah*, and his descendants followed in their holy ancestor's footsteps. They, too, maintained a high level of holiness with regard to guarding the bris. The main condition for maintaining this high level of holiness is purity of thought. One must also guard one's mouth and tongue [from speaking unclean words]...

This is the meaning of the words we sing in the *zemiros* of Shabbos: "*Kol shomer Shabbos mechallelo secharo harbeh me'od al pi pa'alo* — Everyone who guards the Shabbos from being profaned, his reward is very great, commensurate with his deeds."

The word kol, everyone, is a codeword for the tzaddik who guards and maintains the Shabbos (which represents the bris-covenant of the circumcision) from becoming defiled. The reward of such a person is very great, commensurate with his deeds. He is able to activate tremendous good [in Heaven] because his words [i.e., prayers] are heeded above.

Yeshayah alluded to this when he said: "Happy is the mortal who does this [zos], the person who holds fast to it [to maintain its purity], who guards the Shabbos and does not profane it, and who guards his hand [*yad*] from doing any evil" (*Yeshayahu* 56:2). The word *zos*, "this," is a codeword for the Shechinah. The person who holds fast to it [to maintain the purity of the circumcision] is the tzaddik, the righteous person. Only he is worthy of bringing about the supernal union of the Holy One and His Shechinah, for he guards the Shabbos and does not profane it, and Shabbos represents the covenant of circumcision.

Conversely, it is written, "Thus says Hashem to the *sarissim* who guard My Sabbaths [again, Shabbos refers here to the *os bris*]: 'They have chosen what I desire and hold fast to My covenant [as stated above], and I will give them in My House and in My walls a memorial and a name [*yad v'shem*], better than sons and daughters. I will give them an everlasting name which will never be destroyed' " (*Yeshayahu* 56:4–5). This is similar to what is written about Moshe: "In all My House, he is My most trusted servant" (*Bemidbar* 12:7)…

This is why the Torah uses the expression "*kein dovrot*" — "The daughters of Tzelafchad have a just claim [literally, 'they speak rightly']," and "*Kein dovrim*… — The tribe of Joseph's descendants have a just claim [they speak rightly]." The root of *dovrim* is an expression of leadership, as in the verse "*Yadber amim tachteinu* — He will subjugate nations beneath us" (*Tehillim* 47:4). It is incumbent on the leader of the generation to be perfect in the aspect of purity and in the aspect of the perfection of speech. [As mentioned above, the two always go together.] Only through the power of pure speech can the tzaddik draw goodness down [from Heaven] for the children of Israel.

This connection is strengthened ever further in the verse "These are the generations of Yaakov, Yosef…" (*Bereishis* 37:2). Yaakov and Yosef together are considered one holy body. This is why Yosef is identified with guarding the bris as brought in the Holy *Zohar* and in the holy books of the Kabbalah… Yaakov, on the other hand, represents the perfection of speech, as it is written, "*V'aviv shamar es hadavar* — And his father [Yaakov] guarded the matter." The word *davar*, which also means "word," indicates that Yaakov, the leader of the generation, attained the perfection of speech.

Thus, this is the meaning of "They may marry anyone who is good in their eyes as long as they marry within their father's tribe":

This alludes to the fact that the beginning of guarding the bris is in the [guarding of] the eyes... Because the family of Yosef were experts in guarding their eyes, lest they look upon something evil from the sitra achra [the force of evil], the eye of the *sitra achra* had no control over them. No one could look upon them with an evil eye, G-d forbid.

This is why it is written, "They may marry anyone who is good in their eyes." These holy women may only marry those who guarded the *bris kodesh*. It would simply be unthinkable for them to marry anyone less holy than these great tzaddikim of the tribe of Yosef.

This is the meaning of the very next verse, "The hereditary property of the Israelites will thus not be transferred from one tribe to another, and each person among the Israelites will remain attached to the hereditary property of his father's tribe." This means that the *shefa* [flow of abundance and goodness] will never turn away from them. This *shefa* is called "*nachalah*," inheritance, from the holy name *NaChaL* [the initials of the words "*Notzer Chesed La'alafim*," and "*Nafsheinu Chikra L'Adonai*," and "*L'hadlik Ner Chanukah*"]." This flow of abundance and goodness will not be transferred to go to a *mateh acher* [literally, "another tribe"], referring to the fact that it will not go to the sitra achra, the side of evil. Due to its extra holiness, it requires extra protection against the external [evil] forces, lest they [derive their sustenance from the source of holiness].

This is the meaning of the words of the *zemiros* we saw above: "commensurate with his deeds" — through the deeds of the *tzaddik yesod olam* [the righteous of the generation] — "each man in his own camp and each by his own banner." Again, in the merit of maintaining the holiness of the bris, abundance and goodness will flow solely to the camp of the children of Israel. This is the meaning of "Draw Your loving-kindness upon those who know You, and Your righteous charity to the upright in heart" (*Tehillim* 36:11), as I have explained elsewhere.

Date: July 23, 2006
From: Nadia & David Matar
To: Chana Besser
Subject: Re: Tiferes Shlomo on why Israel is under attack

As I understand it:

Israel is under attack cause Jews are punished for the crime of giving away parts of Eretz Yisrael willingly, and Hashem makes sure that we are forced to go back to those beloved parts of our homeland that we so treacherously abandoned.

We left Lebanon willingly — we are attacked from the north and obligated to go back.

We left Gaza willingly — we are attacked from the south and obligated to go back to Gaza.

Eretz Yisrael is screaming out: "Do not abandon me because each time you abandon me...Jews are being killed."

May Hashem protect you, the IDF soldiers, and all of am Yisrael from the folly of our blind, deaf, and dumb political non-leaders and may we go back to all parts of Eretz Yisrael, expelling all Arab enemies — for only then will there be peace.

be strong

nadia matar

Date: July 23, 2006
From: Chana Besser
To: Nadia & David Matar
Subject: Re: Re: Tiferes Shlomo on why Israel is under attack

Thanks Nadia,

I've always admired your courage and love for our land. Never thought I'd be on the end that needed the chizuk. Nadia, yes, you're right. And the Tiferes Shlomo is certainly right, too. He says in another writing that guarding the bris is so difficult that a man cannot succeed in this until he has already perfected himself in all of the sefirot above Yesod: in Chesed, Gevurah, Tiferes, Netzach, and Hod.

Rav Natan Gamedze once gave over from Rebbe Nachman the same thing but in more encouraging language. If I can remember correctly from his class in Tzefat in the name of Rebbe Nachman, once a man is able to guard the bris, then all the other middos will come much easier.

Your issue, Nadia, is the land. All these things are simultaneously important and intertwined. We would not have fallen out of love with our Holy Land had we held to our previous exalted level of shomer habris and tznius.

I quote from Simchah H. Benyosef, author of The Light of Ephraim. I asked the same question you are addressing here in different words when I met this Torah scholar and author in Jerusalem last year. The answer: "Guarding the bris is the penimiyus, the inner reason. All the other critical rectifications are the outward 'symptoms' of it needing rectification." That includes love for the land, guarding our speech, honesty in business, keeping Shabbos, and all the mitzvos — all the big ones, plus more.

I twice heard Rebbetzin Jungreis speak in Manhattan at Heneini Center. It was in the weeks of parashas Noach and Lech Lecha, 1993. She said that when people are not being pure in their homes, then there is robbery out on the streets. Don't think that because you are doing something in privacy, behind closed doors, you are not spiritually affecting the universe. You are.

So everybody is right.

I believe that if we perfect ourselves in loving our land, we will not be saved by that mitzvah alone. If we perfect ourselves in shomer habris, then ALL the rectifications will come quickly and easily.

blessings,

chana

Date: July 23, 2006
From: Ahuvah Gray
To: Chana Besser
Subject: I'm davening

Shalom Chana,
I am davening for your safety. We each have different tafkids in life. May Hashem continue to strengthen you and all the others.
All the best!

Date: July 23, 2006
From: Chana Besser
To: Ahuvah Gray
Subject: Re: I'm davening
Cc: Tzefat under Fire list

Ahuvah,

I've heard you say tehillim. I'll match your tehillim against their "til-im" [missiles] any day. Your prayers, the prayers of all of my friends and family, and the prayers of so many hundreds of thousands of Jews who have never even been to Israel, who don't even know anyone in Israel and are praying for us and sending money, doing all sorts of projects, whatever they can think of, just because they love us so much — all this is precious to Hashem.

May He see fit to eradicate evil from the world in the merit of all the prayers and tzedakah and chesed.

love,

chana

[P.S. If you haven't already read Ahuvah's book, My Sister, the Jew, you're depriving yourself.]

Date: July 23, 2006
From: Yaffa Smolensky
To: Chana Besser
Subject: Why we don't leave

People have written from the States and asked, "Why don't you leave? It's dangerous."

Answer: This is our home. Most of our families, on Moshe's side and mine, perished in the Holocaust. They dreamed of an Israel that didn't exist then. We are the embodiment of all of our deceased relatives and we have the privilege of living in Israel. Their dreams live in us. We must hold the Land; we must stay in our city and not give the victory to the enemy, not let them think that they drove us away. We are Jews and our very souls are connected to this precious land that our enemy wishes to take from us. Not to occupy the land to make their own "country," but to destroy us completely. We must be the first line of defense because, G-d forbid we fall, the rest of the world is next. So we stay...we pray. We ask for your prayers and support as well.

Day 12

Date: July 24, 2006 07:40:45
From: Malka
To: Chana Besser
Subject: Thinking of Tzefat in Melbourne

My name is Malka and I lived with my family in Tzefat from 1989 to 1997. We got married there. Three of our children were born there. We lived in the Old City near Chernobyl Shul. Now we are — temporarily — residing in Melbourne, Australia, longing to go back home as soon as our financial situation allows it.

I cannot tell you how much I value the holy work of communicating you are doing. It has been painful to be so far away in a time like this. Instinct says that we should rush home and add our energy to the incredible work that is being done by all those who have the courage to stay. Having children, I have to admit that even if I had the money to come, I would not consider it responsible to enter a war zone, Hashem having put me on the outside in the first place.

Within the circle of my friends here in Melbourne, there is an awakening taking place. Prayers and Torah study are intensifying. Such a deep connection is being created that during Friday night davening in our little shul one really expects the whole kehillah to lift out of this place of galut and be transported by "kefitzat haderech" to Eretz Yisrael. B'ezrat Hashem, we should merit this to happen soon.

Day 13

Date: July 25, 2006
From: Chana Besser
To: Tzefat under Fire list
Subject: Update

Yesterday, Monday, July 24th, was our easiest day so far. But it was at the expense of a bloody day for our soldiers and other cities who got hit harder. All we had in Tzefat was one big barrage of Katyushas midday, then some stray hits throughout the day. I heard only about 10 in all, and no one was hurt here in Tzefat that I know about.

．．．

Shayna Gamedze, Har Nof, has a guest bedroom. They can take a family of 4 w/ small children. If the kids play well, no limit to the stay. Here's your chance to live with royalty. Rav Natan Gamedze would rather give over Torah than talk about himself. You can order the DVD of his first visit home to Swazililand and his life story. The DVD is entitled: The Prince of Light: From African Prince to Orthodox Rabbi. Amazing, inspiring story! Order from www.natangamedze.com.

．．．

Date: July 25, 2006 1:53 PM
From: Chana Besser
To: Tzefat Under Fire list
Subject: Great news

Great news! ALL the children are going to be all right! Michal was released from Rambam Hospital! Hashem is good!

Michal bat Revital

Bat-Tzion bat Revital

Avraham Natan ben Revital

Odel Chana bat Revital

This is the Tzefat Mor family seriously injured the first day of the war. Andy called the hospital today for their status, and they told him that they had all been released. He asked how he could be sure this was accurate. The nurse said, "I handled them myself." The mother is out of the hospital, too. The whole family is together now.

Date: July 25, 2006
From: Martha
To: Chana Besser
Subject: Take care of yourself

Dear Chana,

It has been so good to get so much information, but at what expense? I fear that you are sitting hour after hour receiving and sending messages and perhaps not taking care of yourself as you should. So, I know you do not have time to answer this question from me, but at least answer it for yourself: how are you, my friend? What you are doing is very, very important, but how you take care of yourself is very, very important, too.

Many, many non-Jews are also praying for Israel. There is so much at stake. I know we couldn't possibly understand as you do, but we pray for Jews to have the land that is rightfully theirs, for the parents to be able to raise their children in peace, for all of Israel to be unified under G-d, allowing for individual differences that ultimately make for a beautiful patchwork of faith. I think of it as my grandmother's patchwork quilt — making such a beautiful whole out of so many different fabrics.

You are in my thoughts more than ever. So often I think, I must tell Chana about that after the war... I should make a list so that I remember. But then I think that after the war will be a busy time of praising, thanking, celebrating, and quiet sleep. Please take care of yourself. Please allow time to just rest.

I love you!

Martha

[Martha was my best and only friend from grammar school, a Southern Baptist now living in Biloxi, Mississippi. Last year, I went through Katrina with Martha's family, via e-mail, once they came back to having electricity. Now Martha's family is going through "Katushyas" with me. Who would have dreamed.]

CHANA BESSER

Let's Respect Each Other's Decisions

Some of my Tzefat neighbors were interviewed from their temporary accommodations in the center of the country. They said that everybody who can get away has left Tzefat, that only the *miskeinim* — the unfortunates — are left in town because they have no family, no money, and nowhere to go. I'll make you a deal. I won't judge you for leaving, and please don't judge us for staying. For the record, most of the people still in Tzefat have tons of offers for places to go.

One family of seven made the decision to leave today. They don't want to leave, but their children are too upset to stay. One of their young children has pneumonia, and none of the kids will stay in any room alone. While they were trying to decide, they received no less than three phone calls every day with offers for housing.

A family of nine has been in a bomb shelter almost all of the time since Thursday. That's already a full week. I asked the father how he felt about being in Israel, in Tzefat, for our first war. "I'm thrilled to be here," he said. "I wouldn't be anywhere else." That's a direct quote.

Another family sent their children to relatives out of town, and the parents stayed. But now they are leaving because their children's level of anxiety is escalating. They are so worried for their parents' safety they can't function.

It is harder on those who are not here — they worry or are frightened all the time, wondering what is happening. Those of us who are here know when there is something to be afraid of, so we are worried much less of the time.

There are funds available now, no repayment necessary, to anyone who wants to leave and doesn't have transportation money. It took a few days to organize it, but no one is trapped in Tzefat for lack of money. For those who are afraid to make the dash to the Central Bus Station, *chesed* organizations or the city sends vehicles to the door and drives them out of town for free. There are free cooked *mehadrin* meals available. *Rabbanim* are giving out cash to any family in need, whether they need it to stay or to leave.

Livnot is repairing the electricity and plumbing in the shelters, although the job might take longer than the war will last, and sending volunteers out to the elderly every day with food and assistance. The twenty or more *hesder yeshivah* boys who didn't get called up comprise a big part of the volunteer force. Devorah Leah and other people who know no fear run errands anywhere for anyone who asks them.

If people tell you the stores are all closed, tell them they are wrong. All the basics are available in the first few business hours daily. You don't need to keep a store open all day when there are so few customers.

Ten people died in Israel from traffic accidents last week. The year-to-date Israel death toll from traffic accidents is around 150 people, from January through part of July 2006. Little of that is war related. The death toll from the war thus far is just a bit more than last week's traffic deaths. Keep that in mind and may it help you to relax. Hashem is watching over us. We can't promise you everyone will be OK, but then that is true at all times.

There are no simple formulas about whether to leave or whether to stay. No *rav* in Tzefat is encouraging a family to stay when their desire is to leave. (Well, maybe one.) No *rav* in town is encouraging a family to leave when their desire is to stay. The way you ask the question determines which answer you will get.

Shalom bayis is probably more of a factor in deciding to leave than the missiles. So is *kibbud av va'em*. If one spouse wants to leave and the other wants to stay, and the kids and parents have to crowd together all day in one little room — well, you can imagine the stress. It's a blessing for them if they have a good *rav* whom they both trust and will defer to his advice. If not, good luck. The war inside that safe room is worse than the war outside.

I consulted my Rebbe, Rav Mordechai Twerski, *shlita*. Of course, I didn't call him until Monday.

"Rebbe, I want to stay," I said.

"You can stay. It's going to take a while, at least another two or three weeks, maybe longer. These are *chevlei Mashiach*, birth pains of Mashiach. They are the worst."

A family asked their Rebbe for advice last week. Their children were very upset by the shelling. The Rebbe said: "Tell the children that the missiles can only go where Hashem lets them."

Most of the Tzefat seminary girls and yeshivah boys were called home by their parents. But some have stayed. The bravest of their teachers are conducting a few classes a day. That means at least a mile walk or drive from their homes.

Someone was standing next to a highly respected chassidic Rebbe in Kikar Maginim when he was invited to bring his family to Jerusalem the Shabbos before last. The Rebbe joked and said that the last he had heard, Hashem was still in Tzefat just as much as Hashem was in the rest of Israel.

I'm not staying in Tzefat because I believe that I will not be hurt. I am staying in Tzefat because I believe that what I am doing, communicating essential information to my friends from Tzefat and informing Jews worldwide what is happening here, is important. At least, that's what some people tell me. And I know it inside. This is what I do, and this is what I do well. It comes easily to me, it suits my nature, and it is of use.

Sometimes I get tired of sitting at my computer all day. Sometimes I think I should go visit the shelters or deliver food packages. But the truth is that I am afraid to run around outside. People braver than I are doing that. If I dash to the square and back, about five or six doorways, that's enough excitement for me for the day.

Some people think that if they have *emunah*, nothing bad will happen to them. "You have too much *emunah*," one daughter tells me. She means I lack common sense. Having too much *emunah* has never been my problem. I wish I had *emunah*.

My parents survived the Holocaust. The rest of their family didn't. I know that bad things can happen, believe me I know it. I learned my numbers sitting on my father's lap, tracing his tattoo from Dachau with my finger.

Serving Hashem doesn't mean that you do His mitzvos and then He is good to you. It doesn't mean that you listen to your rav's advice and then you are safe. Serving Hashem means that you do what Your Creator wants you to do and you accept that His judgment is better than yours. It means that you know you can't escape Him if He has an agenda to settle with you. And that you know that He loves you, even when it doesn't seem that way.

 C8   C8   C8

"Hi, Jane." Jane is my sister. She's in Chicago.

"Hi."

"How are you?"

"Why did you call me?" Jane asks.

"What do you mean, why did I call you?" My sister is always happy to hear from me, especially when Katyushas are exploding in Tzefat.

"We just talked."

"We did?" I didn't remember.

"Yeah."

"Today?"

"Yeah."

"When?"

"Oh, about fifteen minutes ago."

"We talked fifteen minutes ago? Before I talked to Julie, I called you? What did we talk about?"

"You told me how hard they shelled today and —"

"Oh, yeah, you went to Phillip's house and —"

"Yeah."

Silence.

Jane laughed first. Just one small, nervous laugh.

Then I laughed. For a second.

Then we both laughed. Longer.

"I'm not tense. I'm taking this stress just fine!"

Gales of laughter, both of us. At least four or five minutes' worth.

Baruch Hashem, my family knows how to laugh together.

So if a Jew can sing a little song, or dance a little dance, or make a little joke, while they are serving their Creator, while they are doing what, to the best of their knowledge and the depths of their prayers and meditations, their Creator wants them to do, then they have fulfilled their purpose in this world.

We gave Hashem a little *nachas*, Jane and I laughing together on the phone through the sirens and the shellings. Lots of Jews, in Tzefat, in Israel, and all over the world, are giving Him lots of *nachas*. He has a lot to be proud of from His Jewish children.

Parts of this essay originally appeared in *Hamodia* weekly newspaper.

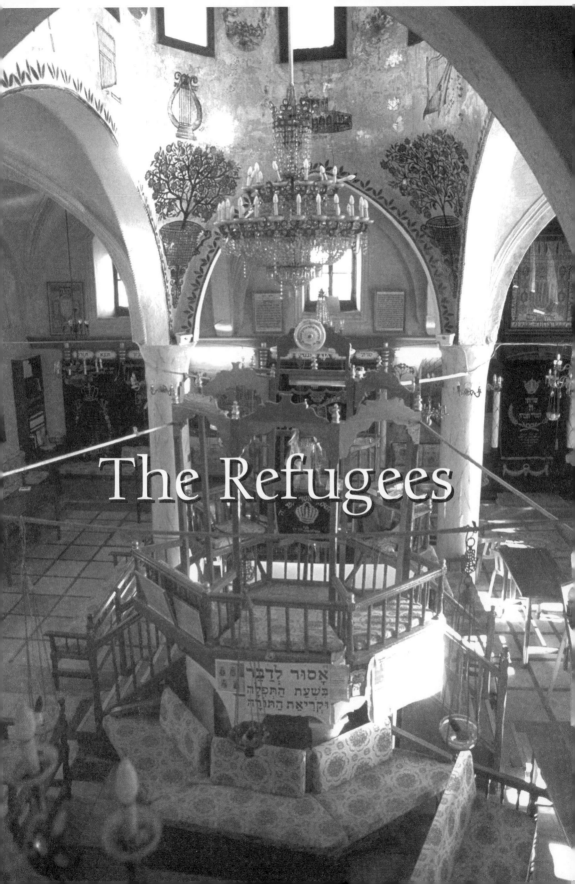

The Refugees

CHANA BESSER

Happy to Help

"Chana, please, come to us today and stay as long as you want."

Many, many invitations would follow from loving and concerned friends, but this call came as soon as the first missiles had fallen.

"For now, I'm staying in Tzefat."

"So just come for today and stay for Shabbos."

"I don't think so. At least, not yet."

Shoshana Cohen respected my decision not to go. She said, "Then send me a family who wants to leave. We have room for about six people."

The next day, *erev Shabbos*, late in the morning, Shoshana called again. "Chana, there are still buses to Jerusalem. You could still come for Shabbos."

The offers continued, as well as frequent calls to check on my well-being. But no matter how many times and how many ways the Cohen family offered to share their home, no one accepted their invitation.

They were trying so hard to find some way to help us directly. The Cohens did some fund-raising for families from the North. But they wanted to do more.

Bein hazemanim, the traditional three-week vacation for yeshivos, came. Yeshivas Pachad Yitzchak was going on vacation.

An organization helping families from the North called the *rosh yeshivah*.

"Families need places to stay. They have nowhere to go. Please, if you'll let us use the dorms and the kitchen, we'll do everything. Can we bring in large families?"

This was the Cohen family's chance to help. They were connected to the yeshivah and were close friends with the Miller family, who had approached the yeshivah through their organization.

Both families went to work. The Millers tackled the fundraising and supplies. There were no sheets, towels, blankets, toys, games, or diapers. They also needed shampoo, soap, and tons and tons of food. The yeshivah was going to take in big families. Tikva Miller worked day and night getting donations of linens, towels, blankets, fans, pillows, and money for kitchen staff and food. The Miller family's son, the Cohens' older children, and two of their friends rolled up their sleeves to set up the yeshivah to receive families. They cleaned, put brand new sheets, pillows, and blankets on beds, and set up the rooms. They hired a cook and helper, and, together with a yeshivah student who volunteered they served two hot meals a day and cleaned up afterward.

Tikva Miller brought in kindergarten teachers and an artist to give the children painting lessons and provided many more activities. One of the guests from the North was a rebbe in a Talmud Torah. He learned with the younger boys every day. On Shabbos, three beautiful, full Shabbos meals were served.

A week after the cease-fire, the Cohens came to visit me in Tzefat with the Millers' son and one of the girls who had worked so hard with them.

"Here's the money we collected for more food and didn't need because of the cease-fire. Use it for Tzefat families who need it."

"That's some wonderful *chesed* you did," I said to Shoshana.

"It's a big *zechus* for us," the Cohen girl said. "We're not soldiers. We can't go out and risk our lives on the battlefield. So we're very, very fortunate that Hashem gave us a chance to help."

"Did you ever get a family to stay with you?" I asked Shoshana.

"No," she answered, disappointed. "We figured out too late what we should have done. One of our married children should have brought their family over to stay with us, and then we could have given their apartment to a family from the North. By the time it occurred to us, the war was over."

They all stayed for Shabbos. At the table, I looked around from face to face. *Tzaddikim*, I thought. Of course, they wouldn't let me say it.

Thank you Hashem, for bringing them to my Shabbos table. Please, let a little bit of their *mesiras nefesh* rub off on me.

BINYAMIN ALEXANDER

Bus Terror

The worst pain for me was on the bus.

Teenage children were vomiting and all the seats in the bus were full. The floor was lined with people sitting and davening.

As the bus meandered down the magnificent hillside toward Meron, the pain started to well up in my heart. My wife Devorah's words from *motza'ei Shabbos*: "Does this mean that we are becoming refugees?" My soul began to weep, as did my eyes.

As the tears rolled into my beard, I looked at the pain on the face of the man sitting next to me on the floor of the bus. I took his hand and gave it a squeeze. "Mashiach must come now," he whispered in pain-filled Hebrew.

"*Im yirtzeh Hashem, chaver,*" was my subdued reply. "G-d willing, my friend." My head slumped forward to the seat in front of me, and I whispered again and again, "*Posei'ach es yadecha u'masbia l'chol chai ratzon* — You open Your hand and satisfy the desire of every living being."

The cell phone rang. It was a friend of ours, now living in Yerushalayim. As she expressed her caring, I began to sob and was unable to respond. Devorah took the phone and they told us that we must come to them.

I couldn't stop thinking that we were leaving the home that we love so well, the holy people who are our friends. What must they also be going through? Did they decide to leave, too? Are they safe? I felt pains in the side of my chest and prayed that they were just from the tension as my wife and I struggled in our own ways to understand what was going on and what was happening. It was hard to keep our equilibrium.

As we left the bus in Petach Tikvah, my heart was breaking.

BINYAMIN ALEXANDER is a fifty-eight-year-old grandfather of eight. He made aliyah to Tzefat from Sydney, Australia, in 2000 and is happily married to his wife, Devorah.

SHIRA YEHUDIT DJLILMAND

Diary of a War Refugee

We have spent the last few days running between bomb shelter and home, each time loaded up with as many basic necessities as possible, at the same time trying to hold and comfort our six small, scared children. Two of them are babies, just four months old. We have slept, all the family curled up together like squirrels hibernating, on the hard concrete floors of the shelter, barely covered by old rugs, for five nights. The noise of the rockets exploding around us is less in the shelter than outside, but still terrifyingly close. The children — and the adults, too — jump every time there is a sudden loud noise and ask each other if that was another one or not.

In between the rushed visits back home for a quick meal and the panicky, frantic race back to the shelter when we hear more explosions, we try to decide what to do. Everyone we speak to is telling us to leave, to take the children to safety. But we have nowhere to go, no family, nowhere that we can just turn up on the doorstep with six children and all our belongings and know that we will be welcomed. And we don't want to leave — we are angry, furious at the thought that Arabs are forcing us to flee from our homes. We want to stay and show them that we are not afraid of them, and that we trust in Hashem to protect us. But the children, they are afraid — they don't understand these arguments of principle and belief. They're just tiny, vulnerable creatures who are scared that they are going to get blown up any minute. Can we put them through this just to prove a point?

More phone calls, more rushed discussions. There's talk of some hotels in Jerusalem giving free rooms to families from the North? Should we go? A friend of ours fled Tzefat for Tiveria. Then rockets fell there, too, and he fled to the States. Is anywhere safe?

Our families call frantically from Los Angeles and England. "Go! Get out already! What are you waiting for? Go stay with your cousin in Beersheva. He'll take you in." But they don't understand. Our cousin in Beersheva is not religious. We couldn't eat there. We could barely stay in their house for more than a few minutes without damaging our children's precious *neshamos*. Who knows what they might see, what they might hear? But here in Tzefat their precious bodies are in immediate danger. What should we do?

Then I remember, with a sudden surge of hope, my first *rebbetzin*, who amazingly lives on the same street as our cousin in Beersheva. She visited us in Tzefat during the Klezmer Festival, two days before the war began. It feels like a lifetime ago, but I remember she invited us, made me promise that we would come and stay with them soon. Perhaps she didn't really mean quite so soon, but just maybe we could go there? I make a hesitant call, hating to ask, but I see the faces of my terrified children before me, and I bury my embarrassment for their sakes.

My *rebbetzin* welcomes my request with open arms. "We were just thinking of calling you. I'm embarrassed that you had to call us first."

Maybe she is just being polite, but we have little choice, so we decide on the spot to go. "We'll be there by evening," we tell her.

Now, how to get there? We call Egged. There is one more bus leaving Tzefat for Jerusalem today at 2 p.m. I pack quickly, and my husband has to go find money for the journey — we have nothing. I feel better now that I have something to do instead of sitting and waiting for the next rocket to explode. I race around, trying to get everything packed. But how much can we carry for eight people? We have to change buses three times, carrying twin babies in a double stroller. I take just one pair of shoes for each child — they'll just have to wear their sandals on Shabbat. For me, just one Shabbat outfit and one other weekday outfit. Can I squeeze in my slippers, or can I manage without them? How many shirts should I take for my husband? And how many changes of clothes for the boys? I tell the children to fill up one bag with as many of their small toys as they can, so at least they're kept busy. My three-year-old has a tantrum because we don't have room for all her dolls.

We ask our neighbor to keep an eye on the house. He is old, Moroccan, widowed — lived through four wars and doesn't care anymore. Nothing will move him from his house, not Katyushas or anything else.

The bus is crowded and tense, full of frightened children, harassed mothers, and fathers trying to be brave. As we leave Tzefat, we see smoke rising from the place where a rocket just exploded.

CB CB CB

We have been in the rabbi's house a week, and already we are starting to feel uncomfortable. How long can a family of eight impose themselves on another family? The rabbi and his family do everything they can to accommodate us, but it's difficult not to disturb them — they have bigger children who don't play loudly or make a mess, and the rabbi has to have his house tidy and quiet so that he can receive people from the community. The children are much wilder than normal; it's almost impossible to control them. I make excuses for them. Actually, they're not excuses, it's the truth — they're still traumatized by what they went through. But maybe people think my kids always behave this badly.

Every day we talk about what to do. Maybe we can go back home? Surely it's going to finish soon? And then we hear the news again — more rockets, more sirens, more injuries and deaths, and more homeless families. We can't go back home yet. Every day we call friends in Tzefat to see what is happening, where the last rockets fell. Were they close to our house? Do we still have a house to go back to? We don't know.

The rabbi tells us the Beersheva Paradise Hotel is giving free rooms to families from the North. Is he trying to help us, or is he trying to get rid of us, or am I being oversensitive? Then we find out the offer is for three days only. We should shlep our entire family to a hotel for three nights and then what? Maybe we could go to Jerusalem? Beit Shemesh? Friends call. One is in Petach Tikva and tells us about a children's camp there. Another found rooms in a yeshivah dormitory, one room to each family. And we hear other stories — of enormous tent cities set up by a wealthy philanthropist, of families stuck in Tzefat with nowhere to go. And all the time the hourly news — more rockets, more sirens.

They are looking after us here. We have free membership to the swimming pool. The boys badly want to go, but the separate hours are only at ten o'clock at night, so we can't take them. We are invited out every Shabbos to huge, luxurious villas, full of fragile vases and precious crystal. I am embarrassed of us in our well-worn Shabbos outfits. We are starting to feel like refugees, poor and pitiful. It is not a pleasant feeling.

A Yemenite family down the street offers us a one-room apartment attached to their villa. We don't know them, we haven't seen the place, but we have no choice. How can we say no? So we accept and I pack up all our possessions yet again. Is this how the people from Gush Katif feel, I think to myself, always on the move?

Baruch Hashem, the apartment, though small, is nice, and at least we have our privacy. We have a separate entrance. We don't have to worry about disturbing our new hosts. They are tzaddikim. They can't do enough for us. It's still hard, though. I don't have any pots, cutlery, cups, anything. If I want to cook, I have to borrow from the family. You get so that you just don't want to ask for anything else. You have nothing, and you have to rely on others for everything. You reach a stage of embarrassment and shame, where you would rather just do without than have to ask for yet more. And still, the hourly news — more rockets, more sirens. Will we ever be able to go home? When?

The children miss their friends, their school, their toys. But they don't want to go back to the "booms," they say. They are difficult. Our four-year-old has started bed-wetting, and our three-year-old will not be separated from her pacifier and comfort blanket. Our five-year-old is angry with the whole world, for destroying his own little world. They refuse to go to sleep unless they can see and hear us both. And they hear the news, too — they don't understand it all, but they understand enough to scare them.

There are lots of Bedouin in Beersheva. The children cling to me when they see them. "Ima, are those Arabs going to kill us?" they ask.

"No, these Arabs are okay," I reassure them, hoping and praying that I'm telling the truth.

My oldest is seven. He thinks a lot about things, turning them over in his mind, and asks deep questions. "Ima," he asks one day, "why do the Arabs want to kill us?"

"Because we're Jews," I answer him simply.

He accepts that for what it is — a fact — and asks no more.

Days, weeks. I lose count of how long we've been here — three weeks, four? We live in a kind of in-between time. It's not schooltime and it's not holiday either. It's just a nothing time, waiting to see what will be. I'm so tired. I want it all to stop. I want to take my poor frightened children back to our pokey little apartment and persuade them that everything is all right and nothing is going to happen to them (if only I could really believe that!).

There is talk of a cease-fire. No one believes it, no one wants it, and no one believes it will last, but there is — for now — some kind of cease-fire. Should we go home now? I want to be home for Shabbat, and I want to clean my apartment — if it's still standing.

We make the decision to go. The children are excited but scared — and that pretty much is true for us, too. *Baruch Hashem*, our apartment is waiting for us, safe and sound. Very dusty and smelly, but our own little space, just us. It feels good. And now life is slowly getting back to normal. Day-to-day matters take over, as they should — birthdays, bills, homework, shopping. Nighttimes are still difficult. The children have nightmares. They think there's an Arab hiding under their bed, and they wake up screaming. Things are back to normal. But nothing will ever be quite the same again.

SHIRA YEHUDIT DJLILMAND, an Englishwoman, is a freelance writer living in Tzefat with her Persian husband and six small children. She writes poetry, feature articles, and children's stories, including the Yosef Chaim stories featured in Mishpacha Junior, and is a regular contributor to *Mishpacha*. Her work has also appeared in *Horizons, Yated Ne'eman, The Jewish Tribune, Stepping Stones, Heartbeats,* and other publications.

REBBETZIN TZIPORAH HELLER

To Stay or Not to Stay

This is a piece I asked Rebbetzin Heller to write for us. She is very concerned about us and calls frequently. I received this Torah from Rebbetzin Heller via e-mail. It was sent after 3 a.m. motza'ei Shabbos.

The Maharal maintains that the reason Hashem gave us minds, abilities, and talents is to use them. What is accomplished by using our abilities is *not* that we can alter the way things will be, but the *person* who we are. When we do what we have to do, we are a different (hopefully better) person than we would be if we did not have to perfect our *middos* in the real world. An example would be the case of a person who knows intellectually that *parnasah* comes from Hashem, but is facing a tough job market. He has to write résumés, go to interviews, network, etc. If he is continually aware of Hashem's Presence even though he is making *hishtadlus*, the results will be real and evident. He or she will make a *kiddush Hashem* wherever he goes and whatever he does. He will never cut corners or feel inner tension because there is competition (or, worse still, actively try to discredit the competition). This is an enormous test, and the reward is that the *bitachon* that was latent and untested now comes out into the world of action and is not just in his thoughts, but what he actually is.

When people think that their efforts change the outcome of events, and not just change the person they become as they make the *hishtadlus*, then they are essentially taking Hashem out of the picture. Outcomes belong to Hashem; choices belong to us.

When people think that they actually change things, they tend to blame themselves and others when the outcomes are not made to order from their perspective. The truth is, to quote the Talmud, "Hashem has many bears and many lions." He can bring about the fruition of His decrees in many ways. Ninety years ago in America people felt desperate when they found that it was almost impossible to get a job where they could be *shomer Shabbos*. They thought (sincerely) that staying *shomer Shabbos* was a death sentence. As things turned out, most people who were really determined to keep Shabbos, regardless of the hardships entailed, discovered that G-d has many agents and they somehow survived. The Jews who gave up Shabbos reached a point in which they felt that they could control events, and only they could take responsibility for their lives without bringing Hashem into the picture.

It is not always simple to know what surrendering to Hashem means. In the example that I gave above, there was only one credible choice to make — keep Shabbos unless you are literally at death's door. Sometimes it is much harder to know what He wants, because there are two credible choices. A perfect (and tragically relevant) example is whether or not to brave it out in Tzefat at the present time. On one hand, retreating from a battlefield under fire can seem irresponsible and cowardly and seems to demonstrate a lack of trust in Hashem, Who can preserve life just as well in Tzefat as He can anywhere else in the world. On the other hand, we are enjoined to preserve our lives and guard our bodies from harm, since they are the greatest gift that Hashem gave us and they are the means through which we do His will. It is permitted to break Shabbos and even Yom Kippur when there seems to be danger, so what is the point of staying when that option, too, seems irresponsible and seems to trivialize the great gift of life?

For some families, the fact that there are two choices rather than one has been a source of dissent when one spouse finds the first choice to be the one that resonates within him most deeply and thinks that his spouse has no faith in Hashem. In other families, the dissent can be fired by one spouse feeling that their husband or wife does not appreciate the value of life and that Hashem will demand an accounting for endangering themselves. What choice is best?

For those of us who are blessed with having a da'as Torah that they rely upon, the answer is easy. For those of us who don't have that sort of relationship with a da'as Torah, or who often consult with various *rabbanim*, the going is a lot tougher. In the efforts that are made to win the "opposing" spouse over to what one perceives as the only right answer, emotions enter the picture. Choosing to go means that "you are a materialistic fool with no real relationship to G-d." Choosing to stay means that "you are a foolhardy idiot who has no sense of responsibility for your family." A lot of history may come up to complicate the picture. Each family is unique, and the question has to be resolved with a maximum of civility, affection, and regard for the other spouse's sense of truth.

In the end, whatever effect *hishtadlus* has on outcomes, it certainly without exception will have an effect on marriages. May we all be wise enough to say at the end of the day, "I sacrificed my ego," which is the highest sacrifice we can offer Hashem.

CHANA BESSER

Blessing from Above (Hotel Rooms Down Below)

Rebbetzin Sarah Blass called me on Thursday, July 27, in the midst of the war. She's been doing all she can to help Jews from the North of Israel. Someone, in total error, posted a message in Tzefat saying that people who needed to leave Tzefat and wanted to stay in a hotel in Jerusalem should call her. They got the contacts mixed up. She was raising spending money for families, not huge sums for hotel rooms.

So her phone started ringing with Tzefat families asking her for hotel rooms in Jerusalem. After a few calls, she figured out that there had been a miscommunication somewhere along the lines.

So what would most of us do? We would say, "You called the wrong person." At most, we would find out the right person's name and phone number and feel like a tzaddik for giving it out. Sarah told Hashem, "It seems like You are sending me a new job to do for You. But I don't have any hotels for these people. If You want me to help them in this way, please — send me a hotel to put them in." And she went on her way.

Walking down the street, a young man greeted her. "Hi, Rebbetzin! Here, I want to give you money for the needs of the Jews from the North." He gave it to her and asked, "Is there anything else you need?"

"Yes," she told him nonchalantly, "I need a hotel to put them in. Do you have one?"

"Well, as a matter of fact, my father has this big complex in the Old City of Jerusalem near Har Tzion. It's empty now because of the war. Usually it would be full in the summers with tour groups. It has 150 beds all together, and the rooms are all different sizes, everything from three to twelve beds per room. We could squeeze in fifteen if we had to. Let me call him."

He hung up and gave Sarah the good news. "He says you can have it for two weeks, for free — 150 beds. He'll have it clean for you by tomorrow noon, Friday, so people can come in before Shabbos."

"Sarah, that's great!" I told her.

"Yes, I just listened to what my husband teaches all the time. He says that the *berachos*, the *shefa* (bountiful blessings), are always being poured down from Above. We just have to open up ourselves to receive them. People want to be loved, but they don't believe anyone would ever love them, so they aren't open to being loved. People need money desperately, but they don't believe that Hashem will send it to them, so they walk around closed and won't receive it. There are invisible pipes flowing constantly with all the *berachos* that we need and want. We just have to align our vessels under the pipes, because if our vessels aren't in the right spot, they don't get anything. And if our vessels have holes in them, then they can't hold anything. So I decided to listen to him, and I opened my heart to receiving what I needed in order to do this *chesed*. I figured if people were calling me, there must be a reason that Hashem let that 'mistake' happen, because Hashem doesn't make mistakes."

CHAVA RACHEL SABAN

A Little of Our Story So Far

It is with great hope and longing for everlasting shalom for all the world that I write this.

I know you are all very concerned about our safety and well-being, so I ask that you do at least one thing, and that is to send only your positive thoughts and visualizations toward us and all of the people of Israel. Imagine us all living in a world of peace! This can be very hard to do at this time, but it is so powerful and crucial and a way to really help if you're wondering, what can I do to help?

We have been staying with our dear friends in the Old City of Jerusalem. They are providing us with a safe refuge and have taken us in like family. Our children play together all day and the mess is unbelievable — eight kids under eight years old expressing themselves exuberantly and creatively, and half of them still showing traces of post–traumatic stress. All get along except for Daniel and Serach, the near two-year-olds, who must be watched constantly for who will make the first strike. We feel so blessed and grateful to be here, alive, in the heart of the whole world, the headquarters of prayer, and we are all praying with great intensity and as much as possible. The children can't help but hear and learn about the mechanisms of the physical war, but they're learning how to fight with words of prayer and acts of kindness.

Thousands gathered to pray together at the Western Wall, and we heard great rabbis of our time crying out psalms from the depths of their hearts, their sobs of prayer broadcast for all to hear. The community here has donated beautiful clothes, food, and money for us, since we left Tzefat quickly, exhausted from missiles going off. It was impossible to take all we needed. We are witnessing continual acts of kindness and unity from our fellow Jews. A family here who would have received up to $2,000 for a month's sublet has donated their apartment to us for the next month!

In the beginning, the war was still "over there" — they were hitting the army base near Mount Meron, and it felt abstract to us. Then they started hitting the town, and the first hit was (ironically) the largely Arab-attending community college on the street above us. That one was really loud and shook our house. We looked at each other and said, "We'd better get into a shelter."

I'm certain Yosef and I faced our greatest fears that day. At some points, I was never so scared in my life. Our street got two close hits while we were there, which broke much of our glass. None of us got hit by the flying glass, *baruch Hashem*, but it sure was loud. It also blew the hinge off our front door and cut our phone line.

At that point, Yosef heard a missile fly right over his head as he stood in our yard, only to hear a shocking silence afterward. Miraculously it didn't go off. There was so much shelling we were afraid to leave as much as we were afraid to sit in our house. In the end, we stayed for Shabbos. That Shabbos taught me the deepest spiritual lessons of my whole life. I traveled to the very edges of my faith in G-d and was forced to examine my beliefs exhaustively. Every time a bomb exploded I had to remind myself that G-d is here and in control. I had to continually reawaken myself to pray and beg the Creator to spare our lives, explaining in great detail how much we want to live, to serve and to give. At the same time I had to accept the possibility that my version of good might be different from G-d's and nullify myself to the Creator's plan for revealing ultimate good. I learned to separate my body's visceral reaction to the sounds of war and gain control over my mind/soul, repeating to myself, *"Ein od milvado* — There is nothing but G-d."

On Shabbos morning we attended a bris milah at our neighbor's house, crying out, *"Shema Yisrael!"* while rockets flew overhead. At night, the only way I could fall asleep for a few hours was by singing prayers from *Tehillim* over and over. In the end, we felt that, even though G-d was with us, it would be a courtesy to just get out of the way. He wants us to care for our safety.

We don't know how or when this will all end. At times I long for the musical instruments we had to leave behind, for our house full of our own things, for "normal life," yet most of the time I feel detached from these worldly possessions and called to a much higher purpose than ever before — to real prayer.

> CHAVA RACHEL SABAN sings, writes songs, teaches music, and raises a family. She has lived in Tzefat since 2001. Her six voice and violin CDs are available at www.chavasmusic.com and www.cdbaby.com.

JOHANNA YAFFE

Excuses

I had a good reason for leaving — didn't I?
The third Katyusha of the war landed across the street from us —
didn't it?
Our building doesn't have a shelter — does it?
We live on the top floor facing north — don't we?
I needed a vacation, badly — don't I?
My sister-in-law invited us to visit her — didn't she?
We were planning to go away that weekend anyway — weren't we?
We did stay for the first six days — didn't we?
My husband said, "Once we leave we have to stay away" — don't we?
It's all outside of our control — isn't it?
The halachah says, "You musn't put yourself into a place of
danger" — doesn't it?
At least we get to spend some time with the family — don't we?
It's only going to go on for the Three Weeks — isn't it?
I'm not really afraid to go home — am I?
Everyone else has left — haven't they?
It was my husband who wanted to leave — wasn't it?
If I'd been alone, I would have stayed — wouldn't I?
I didn't really want to run away — didn't I?
I wasn't a coward for leaving — was I?

JOHANNA YAFFE moved to Israel in 2000 from an assimilated
lifestyle in a small English countrytown. A year later, at the age of
forty-eight, she became religious and married for the first time. She
loves living in Tzefat, enjoys the Tzefat Women's Writing Group,
and strives to continue to develop herself through her writing.

ESTHER RUBENSTEIN

Listening with Your Heart

Before we had the slightest inkling that war would soon overturn our lives, Rabbi Hoffman came to Tzefat on his yearly teaching vacation.

Rabbi Henoch Dov Hoffman comes every summer from Denver, Colorado. All year we wait for for those ten days. "Peace begins inside," he told us on the first day. "Peace with G-d, peace within yourself, then peace with your own community. Only then does it move to larger scales." Three days later the missiles began ripping through Tzefat. They tore apart more than our homes and our lives. They shredded what we love most in Tzefat: our peace.

Tzefat, the dreamy mountain town, slightly separated from the world... There are all types in Tzefat, from chassidic to atheist, from Russian to Ethiopian. We try to accept one another as we are, give people space and time so they can grow, or at the very least give people compassion.

When the missiles hit, everyone reacted differently. It did not matter what group you were affiliated with — everyone made different choices. Some left immediately, some stayed a while and then left, others stayed no matter what. And there were others who had left and came back.

But something else started shaking us up besides the rockets. Dissent rumbled its way below the surface of our minds. Most of us could not help judging one another, if only a little bit. And only sometimes. Even husbands and wives, or perhaps especially, began to argue about whether to stay or leave. So on top of all the other terrors and pressures, the war punched tiny holes into our peace. But, in truth, we were really struggling with our own inner peace of mind.

Each of us struggled with what we understood to be "the right thing to do." I know I did. When the first Katyusha hit, leaving Tzefat was the last thing on my mind. My sister-in-law called and told me I could come to their house. I told her Tzefat was my home. Did they leave Jerusalem when the suicide bombers were blowing up buses?

Then a missile screeched over my head. I was upstairs hanging laundry, enjoying the beautiful sunset over Mount Meron. I had just stepped into the hallway to get more wash. I had never heard that whistling before, didn't understand what was happening when glass shattered and gathered at my feet. I could do nothing but cover my head and wait for the next thing to happen. It did, with a *boom* that shook my whole house. We found out later that two houses behind me my neighbor had just called her children in and closed the door. The Katyusha exploded in the courtyard where their children had just been playing.

I escaped to our unfinished basement, where I saw my teenage son come running home, his face white. "I saw one flying overhead in the street." His voice trembled. My husband ran out to see where it had hit and came back to tell me that a neighbor was hysterical. Shrapnel from the Katyusha had blown through her door as she sat at her kitchen table, hit the wall beside her, and bounced off...missing her, not once, but twice. After fifty-eight years of quiet in Tzefat, this was war.

My husband, my son, and I bunked down in the apartment downstairs. No workable kitchen, no shower, a bathroom across an open courtyard, but at least the back bedroom was underground.

My son decided to leave the next morning for his brother's home in Beit Shemesh. My husband was not going anywhere. I wavered, even though much of my street was emptying out. *Still*, I thought, *we can't all leave Tzefat. This is Eretz Yisrael, not Germany*. I decided to stay, at least for Shabbos, to see how things went. Maybe it would all be over in a few days.

Something wove its way into my mind from our learning of the past few days. The Eish Kodesh, the Warsaw Ghetto rabbi, had been offered a visa to another country during World War II. But he chose to stay with his people.

"What's the difference if you give up part of yourself or all of yourself?" he wrote more than once. "We must keep our integrity, our faith." Maybe I would learn something I needed by staying.

ભ ભ ભ

Friday night, while sitting down to our Shabbos soup, another Katyusha screeched overhead. That same horrible whistling, that pounding fear, the *boom*, and then the silence. This one landed two houses to our right. No one was hurt, thank G-d. They had left before Shabbos.

That's when I knew. I could not go on living like this. Stuck in small quarters, terrified every time I had to go outside to use the restroom or upstairs to cook or shower. I knew that I would begin to feel more and more choked, afraid to go out, paranoid of every blast in the distance. Did one get used to this? Perhaps, but with an offer to go to the center of the country, the price of my sanity was too high to pay — for me, at least. And though my husband didn't want to go, I decided that my choice would have to be different.

The indecision, the tugging toward both sides, goes on in most of us. We who want to do the right thing struggle with ourselves. Finally, when we do make a decision, whatever it is, we often project the "wrong choice" on to others who have chosen differently. So those who stay are "risking their lives unnecessarily," and those who leave are "deserters" or "lacking in faith."

But sometimes we have to listen a little deeper to what G-d is telling us. Everyone is unique, and everyone's situation is unique. If we don't accept all the parts of ourselves, and those who are part of our lives, how can we come to a decision we can live with?

When we come to understand that each person has his personal *tikkun*, we can answer a different question — not what is the one and only right thing to do (I am not referring here to halachah or rabbinic rulings, which, in this case, were different from different *poskim*), the real question is, what is G-d asking of me right now, in this situation? It is certainly not an easy thing to answer.

For me, personally, my answer hit me in my guts. I knew what I had to do.

When my son had insisted on leaving earlier, I had to accept that this was what he had to do. And when my husband decided to stay, though I did not like it because I would be worried, I understood. This was what he needed to do.

Still, we are at war, and I knew that there is a personal *tikkun* here for each one of us. Being out of my home became a big challenge for me, and I found myself, like so many other refugees, uncentered, nervous, and missing my home.

My personal work became the work of focusing, of trying to find *HaMakom* wherever I was, of appreciating the goodness of the people who opened their homes to me, my son, and eventually my husband, of trying to fill my day with something useful to others. Keeping my inner peace, and my peace with G-d, has become a less intense challenge than if I had stayed in Tzefat, but an ongoing and perhaps more subtle part of my own stretching.

> ESTHER RUBENSTEIN has raised a family in Tzefat for nearly three decades. She writes freelance for religious publications and teaches creative writing.

ESTHER HELLER

"Is This a War, Mommy?"

We woke this morning to the sound of Katyushas falling in nearby Meron. "Can they hit Tzefat?" my daughter wanted to know.

"It's more dangerous to cross the street," I reassured her. "More people get killed being hit by cars than by falling missiles."

Standing on our porch, we can see the smoke rising over the Meron mountain range. Firefighting planes fly overhead on their way to extinguish the fires. With binoculars we follow the planes and helicopters.

Suddenly there is a short, loud blast. "Is that a bomb?" another daughter asks.

"It sounded like the garbage collection," I answer.

"Is this a war, Mommy?" my younger daughter asks.

"I don't know," I answer honestly. "But it's still more dangerous to cross the street or drive in a car."

My mother calls. "Did you know that Rosh Pina was hit?" she asks.

"No," I answer, knowing what she will say next.

My mother doesn't seem to realize that we live closer to Meron, which has been hit many times. I decide this isn't the right time to inform her.

"This is too close," my mother continues. "I want you all to come to Netanya and stay with us until things quiet down."

"Thanks so much, Mom, but really, we're fine. You see, they are targeting military bases and we don't live near one." (The nearest one is at least a ten-minute drive away.)

My mother sounds dubious, but she drops the subject. For now.

I've just put down the phone when it rings again. It's my husband calling. "Did you hear a loud noise a few minutes ago? That was a Katyusha hitting Meron."

Well, I guess it wasn't a garbage pickup, after all.

My husband calls again. "Tell the children that driving in a car is statistically much more dangerous than..."

"I know, I told them already."

My older daughter runs a camp for twelve- to fourteen-year-old girls. They were supposed to take a trip next Tuesday and she wonders if she should cancel it. "Why don't you wait and see?" I advise.

Next week we have a family *seudah*, a *siyum* scheduled in honor of our daughter's bas mitzvah. Family members from all over Israel are expected to come. Will they still come? I wonder. Will they feel safe? Then I think about where my family lives. My sister-in-law lives in Jerusalem with its many terrorist attacks. My cousin and her family live in a small, isolated settlement past Efrat. My parents live in Netanya where they have had some miraculous near misses with terrorist bombings. And my married nephew lives in Kiryat Arba, which adjoins Hebron. No, I don't think they will hesitate to come.

ଔ   ଔ   ଔ

By afternoon everyone was home. Due to the fast (17 Tammuz), the girls didn't have day camp and my son returned home early from cheder. "Can they hit Tzefat?" my children wondered.

"I think there would be an air-raid siren first," I answered, remembering the Gulf War.

The children spent the afternoon looking out the window, watching the firefighting planes futilely trying to douse the forest fires on Mount Meron. Occasionally we heard Katyushas exploding around Rosh Pina.

Suddenly there was an explosive sound like nothing I'd ever heard before in my life. My kids started screaming and crying and wisely ran into the inner bedroom away from the window. "It's OK," I soothed them in a shaky voice. There was another explosion even closer, and then another one so unimaginably earsplitting, so close-sounding, that we seemed to feel it rather than hear it. Unable to control myself, I screamed. It felt good to scream, but I stopped myself immediately, afraid of scaring my children. They looked incredibly scared even without my input. Some were crying, some were holding on to each other. My six-year-old didn't utter a sound, but her whole body was one big tremor.

"Let's go downstairs," I told them.

No one moved. We live in an old stone house in Tzefat's Artists' Quarter and you have to go through the courtyard to get from the upstairs to the downstairs. No one wanted to go outside.

Somehow we found ourselves downstairs in the innermost room, my mother-in-law's bedroom. She looked shaken, too, and I worried how she would handle this. I went back upstairs to collect a few things, and my son followed after me. Suddenly we heard an air-raid siren. My son and I ran down the stairs and joined the rest of the family. Aren't the sirens supposed to sound *before* the bombs?

Instinctively, I started to pour myself a glass of water, then stopped. Today was a *tzom*! I had almost forgotten.

After the missiles, everyone was very shook up. It took a long time till we felt calmer. Some of my children were sitting on the floor cutting and gluing. It was so nice to see them distracted enough to work on an arts-and-crafts project. Then they happily ran over and showed me what they had made: missiles! Using cardboard cylinders and cut-out triangular shapes, they had made convincing replicas. All I needed now was for them to fly them around the house!

My six-year-old seemed the most upset in her own quiet way. Too quiet. I tried to make her feel better. "When Mashiach comes, we'll all go to Yerushalayim. Which Shabbos dress do you want to wear then?"

Her face lit up. "Can I wear my new dress that we're saving for Rosh HaShanah?"

"Yes, honey, yes."

We started getting food ready to break the fast, when suddenly we heard a series of short staccato booms that felt like they were right near our house. It sounded like amplified, robust, and malevolent thunder.

Wordlessly, we all ran into our "safe room," the one windowless room of our house. My seventeen-year-old was standing there already in the middle of davening *Shemoneh Esrei*. She was weeping, her face covered by her siddur. I called my husband. Thank G-d, he was at shul with my son. My married daughter didn't answer her phone. My children opened their *Tehillim*. I paced around the small crowded room.

"Let's get out of here," the children begged when they could stop crying long enough to speak.

"Abba asked the Rebbe what we should do," I reminded them. "We are just waiting for the *gabbai* to call with his answer."

I decided to call the *rebbetzin* and update her on our situation. By now, I knew that many of the missiles had been very close: one in Tzefat's Old City and two in the Artists' Quarter, where we live. One missile hit a house and injured a mother and her children. A child was feared trapped under the rubble. Another missile had exploded across the street from our roof. A man on a motorcycle was killed.

I explained to the *rebbetzin* these new developments as well as the tremendous fear my children were experiencing. "I think we should leave, for our children's sake," I explained, "but I also fear being out on the open roads. What should we do?" The *rebbetzin* assured me she would call me back as soon as possible.

I kept trying to reach my daughter and son-in-law. I knew that the sealed room they were in didn't have good reception, but

I still kept trying. They were thinking of taking the bus that night to my son-in-law's parents in Jerusalem, but were afraid to be out on the streets.

We broke our fast on orange soda and homemade pizza that one of my daughters had found the composure to make. We could barely eat a few bites. The children slept in their *bubby*'s room, the room we hoped was safe because it had no windows.

My husband came home from shul. There had been explosions during *minchah*, and the two Hatzalah members ran out of the minyan to help. On his way home, my husband walked over to see the damage on the street above our house.

One of the rockets sounded as if it had flown right over our house. It had. My husband saw the hole in the street where the man on the motorcycle had been killed. A car had been crunched, and there was broken glass everywhere.

Meanwhile, at home, the children wanted to know if we were leaving. I told them not tonight, but maybe we would leave before Shabbos since it wouldn't be *oneg Shabbos* to remain. I did not feel afraid, only worried about my children's fear. When they were asleep, I went upstairs — they were too afraid for me to go upstairs while they were awake — to do the laundry and straighten up. My husband helped me back up all of my computer files.

I looked out over the balcony. The Meron mountains were still on fire. The streets below me were completely deserted. No cars, no people, no streetlights. Our holy city — more like a little village — had been untouched by war or terrorism for many years. Our little town, where progress meant reversing the traffic patterns on the one-way streets.

When I read stories about the Holocaust, I often wonder about those who had the chance to flee for their lives, yet didn't want to leave their homes. How could they choose to stay? How could they not realize what would happen?

As I looked out over the mountains, the stone houses and cobblestone lane, I felt so clearly and so deeply that I did not want to leave my home.

I slept on the living room couch, and all night I heard the

war planes and helicopters heading for Lebanon. Around 3 a.m., I finally slipped into a real sleep. At 4 a.m., the telephone rang. I knew it must be the *gabbai* with the answer from our Rebbe. It was. I woke my husband and he took the phone.

"The Rebbe said we do not need to leave, but if we want to we can. And we can consider it safe to travel if the Egged buses are running." The *gabbai* added: "Give your kids a chance to calm down over Shabbos and don't feel that you have to run back to Tzefat."

I knew how strongly my husband didn't want to leave.

"Why don't you want to leave?" I asked him.

"Because it's letting our enemies win," he answered. "They want to scare us and make us run away from our homes."

But we knew that for the children's sake we should go. It was after 4 a.m. and three of my children were awake. I told them we were leaving in the morning, and for the first time that night they were able to sleep.

At 7 a.m. our phone started ringing again. I called my parents and told them we were coming.

"What time are you leaving?"

"At 11 a.m."

"Can't you come earlier?"

"I'm sorry, we can't. The house is too much of a mess."

"Just leave the house and come!"

"No, I can't do that."

Never have my children been so eager to clean. Without telling them specifically what to do, I saw them all in the kitchen, one girl at each sink, another washing the floor, and my nine-year-old son throwing out the garbage.

What to take and what to leave behind? How long would we be gone? Just for Shabbos? Until Tishah B'Av? Longer? Could it possibly be longer?

"Pack enough for the Nine Days," my seventeen-year-old said, always the one to plan ahead.

My husband only packed for four days. I slipped some extra clothes of his into my suitcase.

"Can I bring my Rosh HaShanah dress?" my six-year-old asked.

"Honey, we aren't going to be gone that long," I reassured her.

"But I don't want anything to happen to my dress," she said with a catch in her voice.

"If something happens to it, I'll buy you a new one."

"But the necklace..."

That two shekel little necklace hanging in a plastic bag on the hanger with the dress. "And I'll buy you a new necklace, too," I added.

Her face still determined and fearful, she said, "But you said that when Mashiach comes, I could wear it..."

"OK, pack it."

My mother called again. One of her friends in Netanya whose grandson was in the army had learned that there wouldn't be any rockets until 10 a.m. Would I please see if the driver could come earlier and just forget about packing and cleaning the house?

My parents' friends are always coming up with these security-related pieces of information, so I can't say this phone call surprised me. I managed to get off the phone without committing myself to anything. I finished the packing for my two youngest and started packing for myself. The night before, my husband and I had backed up all my writing onto one slender CD. Everything I had written till now was on it.

I spoke with a friend on the phone who was trying to decide whether to leave or not. We heard *boom, boom, boom, boom.* "One, two, three, four," my friend counted into the phone as she made her decision to leave. (It was after 10 a.m. My parents' sources were right.) The sound was distinct enough to be near, but not loud enough to be real near. We were becoming military experts fast.

We brought our outdoor plants to our neighbors who live across our small cobblestone lane. They had decided to stay. I gave them our house key and told them if the electricity was cut to please take the chickens in our freezer, cook them, and enjoy them.

I took the clothes off the line. A few items were still wet. I knew I should take them inside, but I didn't. I moved them from the large line to the smaller clothing rack that was covered by an awning. I went from room to room, turning off lights, looking to see if there was anything else we should take. I had one small suitcase of clothing and a tote bag containing a siddur, Tehillim, phone book, the computer disc of my writings, and a book by Rebbetzin Heller. We gathered our suitcases and left. Several shirts, a towel, and some socks were still hanging on the line.

My children ran with the suitcases and piled them into the van. We all got in: my children, son-in-law, granddaughter, mother-in-law, a young couple who was heading for Bnei Brak, and Shari, a girl my married daughter had met the day before while they were both trying to find a bomb shelter.

My husband locked up the house and joined us in the van. "Does anyone see the bag with my tefillin?" he asked. We all searched, the kids nervous that we were sitting stationary in the van. Every row was filled with bags and suitcases of all shapes and sizes. The minutes ticked by. I tried to keep my impatience to myself. *I supervised all the packing and cleaning up of the entire household and he can't keep track of his tefillin*, I thought with wifely annoyance. Then, suddenly, I realized. *This is really hard for him, too. He doesn't scream or cry like the girls or write like me.* Just then, I looked down and there was his tefillin. Right between my daughter and me.

We wound our way out of town, passing the bus stops of Tzefat, each one filled with big families waiting for buses to Bnei Brak and Yerushalayim, their suitcases spread across the ground. Later I heard that the buses had been packed past capacity, the aisles filled with people.

There were no other cars on the road. Other than the bus stops, the streets were deserted. As we neared the highway, we all felt relieved, or, as my daughter described it, "taking a breath without feeling fear." It could have been a vacation that we were packed and traveling for. It was summer, and the kids had brought their bathing suits and hoped to go to the beach. We were going to the welcoming arms of my parents, who would do everything they could to make us happy. We were not like real refugees, *chas v'shalom*. And yet we were leaving our homes unwillingly, for an indefinite period of time. In that sense we could be considered gilded refugees.

We arrived in Netanya, and my parents happily welcomed us into their home. I introduced Shari to my parents, who had no idea that we were bringing someone else. They welcomed her warmly and invited her to stay for Shabbos.

After a peaceful Shabbos, we decided to make as normal a routine as possible for our children. They still seemed anxious and were constantly asking us what was happening.

A close friend who is part of the Sanz community in Netanya helped us arrange day camp for my three youngest girls and put us in touch with the principal of the cheder. Although we are not Sanzers, they warmly accepted us. I thought my girls would be too shy to go somewhere that they didn't know anyone. I thought I would have to work hard to convince them. I was surprised by how eagerly they took to the idea. I think that their desire for a normal childhood routine overruled any other considerations. My nine-year-old, however, knew he would not like the cheder. "Let's just go meet the rebbe," my husband told him. "You don't have to stay."

Would they make friends? My girls don't know Yiddish. Would they understand what was going on?

When I arrived to pick them up, my twelve-year-old was exchanging phone numbers with another girl. That night, the phone rang a couple times for my fourteen-year-old. It was her new friends calling.

"Did you understand what your counselor was saying?" I asked my six-year-old. She shook her head but had a big smile on her face. I guess understanding words isn't everything. The happiest of all was my son, who loved the cheder. It may seem like a very small thing to take the time to make some phone calls to help another person or for a child to befriend the new child in the camp. They are not small things.

When I write these accounts, I feel like I am connecting with Yidden everywhere. We are one people, one heart. During 9/11, I had such a strong need to know and to feel what those close to the destruction were experiencing. I imagine that you, now, feel the way I did then.

> ESTHER HELLER is the director of The Jewish Writing Institute, www.jewishwriting.com. She is fiction editor at *Binah* Magazine and writes for various publications. This essay first appeared in *Hamodia* weekly newspaper.

DISPATCHES FROM THE FRONT LINES

The War
Continues

The Bostoner Rebbe Speaks about the War

Transcribed and adapted from an address given by Rabbi Yitzchak HaLevi Horowitz, the Bostoner Rebbe, on Wednesday, July 26, 2006 (Rosh Chodesh Av 5766)

We are in the midst of a major war. And every day that we have to face it, there are more and more casualties. What do casualties mean in terms of the individual Yid? It is something that must awaken in us the feeling that we must do something more. It is not just another session of *Tehillim*. We have to make sure that we say the *Tehillim* with all of our hearts because we realize the consequences of what is happening.

It's hard to think about the consequences, G-d forbid. But this is a very serious matter. From my point of view, from hearing the news and reading about what the government, the authorities, say about it, I feel that we have already lost the first phase of the war. If the enemy can strike wherever he wants at any time of the day or night, we have lost the war. If the enemy can beat the Jewish army and are able to potentially kill civilians, if the Hezbollah can succeed in a hand-to-hand skirmish, if they have the ability to kill our soldiers, if they can beat the sophisticated Israel army, we are in great trouble.

I want to mention a little incident, a terrible incident, that I never repeat because it hurts too much. It takes too much of a toll on the person who tells it.

We had in our midst, in Poland just before World War II, a great, great tzaddik, the author of the *sefer Chovas HaTalmidim*, the Piaseczner Rebbe. Every *talmid* in yeshivah learned his *sefer*, whether he was a chassid or not a chassid. His *sefarim* were popular everywhere. He went *al kiddush Hashem* afterward. When the war broke out, the Piaseczner Rebbe received notice of the first death in his family. Someone told him that, *Rachmana litzlan*, his son had been killed. He said just a few words: "The war is just beginning, but I have already lost my own war."

Appreciate the fact that we, each one of us, to a great extent have lost our war. We've lost those beautiful *Yiddishe neshamos*, those beautiful souls. For what? Because the goyim can't stand the very existence of the Jewish people.

We are suffering on all fronts, in hand skirmishes, in the missiles that they send, and not even sophisticated missiles. So what is there for us to do? When we say *tehillim*, let us realize that we have to do all we can to help those on the front, which is not just Lebanon; it is everywhere — in Haifa, in Tzefat, in Tiberias, in Akko, everywhere... And that we are to do it, not just by saying we are going to be different, but by taking upon ourselves special mitzvos, special things to do because of the terrible tragedy that has befallen us.

There is a *chazal* that says that for each soldier on the front there was one Jewish person in the back of the ranks who prayed and did mitzvos for his fellow Yid. This is now our task: to do that which would make it possible to gain victory over an enemy that knows no limits.

In the three weeks between Shivah Asar B'Tammuz and Tishah B'Av, there are three haftorahs. The first haftorah is "Divrei Yirmeyahu — The words of Yirmeyahu." The second message begins with "*Shimu Shamayim* — Listen, Heaven." The third is

"Chazon Yeshayahu — The vision of Yeshayahu."

Rav Tzadok HaKohen, a great chassidic thinker and tzaddik, says that these three haftorahs contain the following message. The first one begins with *"divrei,"* speech. In times when things are not going well, a Yid must remember to do away with talk that is not proper: *lashon hara, rechilus,* chutzpah. That's *"divrei."*

The second haftorah is *"shimu"* — to hear. Only hear good things. Listen only to that which is proper and not be a party to hearing other things that you should not. That includes the media, of course. Let's be honest with ourselves. So many times we are not doing things with a righteous motive. Let us be honest with *shimu,* with listening.

The third one is the most important. Shabbos Chazon, the vision, the eye. We should control that which affects the eyes and understand that the eye is the most powerful instrument a person has. If we relax our rules on *tznius,* we cause other people to do things that they should not do because of us. When we are careful in our *tznius,* we are not doing anyone else a favor; we are doing ourselves a favor — not to be the *yetzer hara,* not to be the instrument of evil.

In thinking and reflecting on how to go about our job, on what we can do for the people on the front lines, for the people that have been uprooted from their homes, let us remember these three injunctions on speech, on hearing, and on vision.

This brings us to a terrible, terrible episode in our own history. Just a year ago, we read something in the newspapers and we didn't do so very much about it. We read that Jewish communities in the Gush Katif area were going to be uprooted and thrown out of their homes. We went back to our own merry ways and didn't do a thing, didn't say very much, didn't protest it. The end result is...I don't have to tell you. Now you see other Jews being uprooted. You most likely know some people from Haifa, from Tiberias, from Tzefat; they came to your communities uprooted from their life.

Of course, those who did the uprooting of the innocent people of Gush Katif thought they could control the situation in Israel. We can tell people where they should live and where they should not live. We can kick them out when we want to. We can even kick out the people in the cemeteries and throw them to some other place because we can decide where the dead people, even the dead people, should have a place. That was the government's position. But the *Eibishter* tells us, "So you felt that you can kick the Jews out of one block in Eretz Yisrael and you can secure the other block?" And so what we have now is that the other block is also not secure.

You can't make the decision of where it is secure and where it is not secure. You have no right to throw a Yid out of his home in Eretz Yisrael. Only the *Ribbono shel olam* makes that decision.

At least in hindsight, let's reflect on this: I have done something wrong. I have done something wrong by being quiet and by not speaking up.

Tehillim is an instrument of *taharah*, of spiritual purification. When we say and learn *tehillim*, we are involved in an instrument of *taharah*, a very special cleanliness that will make us a better instrument of goodness, a better instrument of truth, a better instrument of positive interaction between man and man. All of that can come about by the *tehillim* we say if we say it with all our hearts, with the *kavanah* that we hope people will give it, to be able to fulfill the *ratzon* of Hashem Yisbarach. And may Hashem Yisbarach send us Mashiach speedily in our time.

REBBETZIN TZIPORAH HELLER

From Pizza to Teshuvah

Transcribed and adapted from an address given at Neve Yerusha-layim on July 26, 2006

This is getting to be, for those of us who were here together at the Bostoner Shul in Har Nof (Jerusalem) last summer, a yearly disaster gathering. Who knows what will be next year? Hopefully Mashiach. But there's a big problem that this is where we're at. We should not be having yearly disaster gatherings.

One of the rebbes from Neve Yerushalayim actually heard this from Rav Moshe Shapiro. He heard that the situation we are in now is not unrelated to what happened last year at this time. We shouldn't think for a moment that what happened last year is unlike, for example, the Inquisition. The only reason the Jews were expelled from Spain was because they were Jewish. The only reason the Jews were expelled from Gush Katif is because they are Jewish. Whatever the Israeli government decided, they decided because of fear of the Arabs. Our enemies among the Arabs don't want us here, in case you didn't notice, anymore than the Nazis wanted us to be in this world. We're not wanted in this world.

It was said that during the Babylonian exile we slept for seventy years. I want you to think about what that implies. Some of us have read about Rip Van Winkle; others have read about Choni HaMe'agel. Imagine waking up and seeing seventy years of your life gone.

Something similar actually happened to someone recently. Some of you may have read about this in the paper. A man named Willis woke up after twenty years of being in a coma state. He thought he was still twenty-two. Imagine discovering that you are forty-two. His whole youth was gone.

It seems there are people who are not just asleep; they are in pre-surgery anesthesia. For them, no matter what happens, life goes on. The biggest question in their lives continues to be "Is pizza better with olives or with mushrooms?" What is it going to take for people to wake up?

Here's a *mashal* of where we're at right now: Suppose you had a neighbor and your neighbor's child was, G-d forbid, run over by a car. People come banging on your door, then you see the ambulance take the child and the mother away, and they tell you, "Pray! Say *tehillim*!" What would you do? Order pizza? No, you would open your *sefer Tehillim* and you would say *tehillim* with all your heart, of course.

Right now, we don't know what's happening in the North. There are lots of miracle stories and there are also tragic stories. We need to turn our attention from pizza to *teshuvah*.

This war is a lot like what I saw during the Gulf War. Everyone wanted to change, but nobody knew how. Nobody knew what to do. I see this now, too. So this time the *rabbanim* have given us specific directions.

Here is a *"kol korei,"* a rabbinical proclamation. We will review it together now.

It begins by telling us that this is an *eis tzarah bnei Yaakov*, a time that is hard on all Jews. We're always referred to as *"bnei Yisrael,"* not *"bnei Yaakov."* Yaakov is the undeveloped state of who we as a Jewish nation could be. This is where we are, at the Yaakov state.

It goes on to say that there is great danger upon us. I want you to notice that nobody is saying there is no danger. Nobody is saying don't worry. We need great *rachamim* (mercy). So if that's the situation, then we have to understand one thing: we can't get *rachamim* without drawing down *rachamim*. And you can't draw down *rachamim* without being a *ba'al rachamim*.

Now the Rambam is quoted. The Rambam tells us that it is a mitzvah from the Torah that whenever things are bad, we have to cry out to Hashem. It's not a nice idea thought up by someone at Neve Yerushalayim or in Boro Park. It is a mitzvah from the Torah. The outcry is to bring the person to *teshuvah*. The outcry is not an end in itself.

Now let us go to the words of our *gedolim*. May they enter into our hearts, bring us to being truly *"bnei Yisrael,"* and protect us:

Rabbinic Proclamation
A message sent by Rav Elyashiv and Rav Steinman, *shlita*:

Klal Yisrael is suffering terribly, and we have nothing to rely on except our Father in Heaven. We don't know the ways of Heaven, but certainly each one of us must search through his deeds.

It is very possible that this is part of what Chazal refer to as "the birth pangs of Mashiach." They explain that what a person should do to be saved at the time of *chevlei Mashiach* is to put efforts into Torah and acts of kindness.

1. Each person should try to strengthen his own commitment to study Torah.

2. We certainly should do everything to see that we at least are not behaving in a way that is the opposite of kindness — that is, we may not bring grief to any individual or to any community. Chazal tell us that Achav's generation worshiped idols, but because they were united, they went to war and won. When there is *machlokes*, this is not the case, may Hashem rescue us! We must try very hard to bring peace to our interpersonal relationships.

3. We know how beloved our Shabbos observance is to Hashem and how much its opposite is despised. Recently efforts have been made to strengthen our resolve to avoid patronizing places that desecrate Shabbos publicly. This is especially true in the cases where using their services doesn't affect human life in any significant way. Unfortunately, there are some segments of the com-

munity that find it hard to give up patronizing places that desecrate Shabbos and rent their premises. This bolsters the attitude that Shabbos is not that important and that it is enough to keep Shabbos in private.

4. We need to work on *tznius*. This is especially important because it says that when there is no *tznius*, the Shechinah "turns aside from you." It is important for us to strengthen ourselves in this.

We are not saying that we know why this suffering has come upon us. Nonetheless, it is certainly true that strengthening ourselves may help turn aside Hashem's wrath.

(Rav) Yosef Shalom Elyashiv
(Rav) Aharon Y. Steinman
20 Tammuz 5766

Day 14

Date: July 26, 2006
From: Chana Besser
To: Tzefat under Fire list
Subject: Baruch dayan ha'emes

> Baruch Dayan ha'emes. We lost 8 soldiers today. A very high price we are paying to eradicate evil. Let it not be in vain.
>
> Gidon ben Yehudit needs our prayers. He is a soldier seriously injured today. I didn't get any other names yet.

Date: July 26, 2006 14:03:19 EDT
From: The Smolenskys
To: Chana Besser
Subject: Lev U'Neshamah

> 8:15 p.m., Tzefat, Israel
>
> Today a prison guard, complete with gun, was supervising some prisoners who have been put to work cleaning out bomb shelters and doing minor repairs. We hope the unused other half of our shelter gets cleaned and painted. They told us that electricity would be installed as well. The part of the shelter we've used has electricity only because the people in the house above the shelter strung an extension cord from an outlet in their house and out the window through an air hole in the wall of the shelter. Creative thinking, yes? Our shelter is BYOB: bring your own bottle...of water and anything else you might need.

The mayor said that about 12,000 of over 32,000 people remain in the city. A large number, he stated, are elderly, infirm, and immobile, and many have no families to care for them. Support from neighbors disappears with their leaving. Police and soldiers canvassed a lot of the city to determine who was in difficulty and how they could be assisted. People here are helping in any way they can. Lev U'Neshama (http://www.levuneshama.org) has people identifying those in need so we can try for another food delivery this coming week. We are also lining up merchants of small, independent stores to supply the staples that are needed for delivery. Our aim is to help those in need and keep the small neighborhood stores open.

A friend who fled with her family decided to collect where she is now living and she called this evening to get our address so a check could be sent. Another man called and gave me e-mail addresses to which I should send appeals under his recommendation. Hope comes from many areas and for this we are grateful on behalf of those of us who are "holding down the fort."

Shalom, Yaffa Smolensky

• • •

Want to learn Hebrew fast?

Rivka and Yossi, wonderful people, would like to host a religious family from the North in their home here in Metar (near Beersheva). They are Israelis, don't speak English, and have hearts of gold.

leah

CHANA BESSER

Wartime Davening

Friday, July 28, 2006
3 Menachem Av 5766

T here is so much to do, so many thoughts to write and share, so many people to call. The tension of the booms masks the tiredness. The body doesn't even know how tired it is. It's often two or three in the morning before I turn off the computer. Last night was a late night.

Now I'm sorry. I can only daven *shacharis Shemoneh Esrei* on time if I skip most of *Pesukei D'Zimrah* and a few verses in *Korbanos*. I remember one opinion cited in Mishnah Berurah not to daven the morning *tefillos* out of order. Do they go up to Shamayim differently if I say them after *Shemoneh Esrei*? Oh, why didn't I make a list of these things to ask my Rebbe? The constant explosions, the anxiety of not knowing how close the next boom might be, and so much to do for others — the list of questions never gets made.

Live dangerously, Chana. Say them out of order. The Shulchan Aruch allows it. Be glad you davened Shemoneh Esrei on time.

The telephone rings. It's Elisheva. "I have leftovers for the chickens, and I'm going out now for a few things. Can I bring them by now?"

"Yes, and I need to run an errand, too."

We decide to go together. The booms have made us two fiercely independent women happy to have a friend to run through the streets with.

A siren blares just as we enter Tzefat's main shopping street — a one-way lane about two blocks long, cobblestoned, cars mingled with pedestrians and fringed with clothing racks and café tables exposed to auto exhaust. We pause for a fraction of a second, look directly into each other's eyes, and continue on at a faster pace than before. "We're in the worst place possible," I say as we half-walk, half-run. "We have storefront plate-glass windows on both sides of us for the next block."

"Have you noticed?" Elisheva says. "The cars aren't stopping for the sirens any more than we are." Drivers continue on, just driving a little faster.

Nothing happened. The danger has passed. We arrive at the newsstand. While we wait, I glance across the street at the regulars sitting outside Angel's Bakery. The two or three café tables are full. Several men are enjoying their *erev Shabbos* midmorning coffee, sweet roll, and cigarette as if there were no war.

Another long, blaring siren brings lots of scared shoppers looking for cover. About twelve people are now crowded together into a space more comfortable for four or five, and everyone is probably as worried about the plate-glass windows as I am.

We stand there with nowhere to look except at Angel's Bakery directly opposite us. The men at the café tables don't budge. They sip their coffee and puff on their cigarettes and look back at us. It is the scaredy cats inside against the fatalists outside, a silent exchange of *hashkafos*. Each side gives the other something to think about.

Nothing explodes close enough to scare us. "I can go on to the pet shop by myself and you can go home," Elisheva offers.

I hesitate. By nature I would leave, grateful for the extra few minutes to accomplish more before Shabbos. *This is no time to desert your friend.* "No, I'm going with you," I tell her. "I can buy some things at Shefa Tov."

This end of the street has a few more stores open. It's much busier than a few blocks down where I live. It feels good to see more people out on the streets. It makes me feel less crazy for staying.

As we walk around the barricaded storefronts and sidewalk where the Katyushas struck on the first day of the war, a lady passes by and I gasp.

How can she dress like that? I ask myself, beginning an internal dialogue that goes on as I walk slowly down the street.

"Chana, twenty years ago you dressed the same way. She doesn't know that she's endangering our lives, just like you didn't know it back then either."

"Say something to her."

"You don't love her. It's forbidden to reprove someone you don't love."

"I do love her. She's a Jew."

"Keep your mouth shut." I end the conversation with myself.

The pet shop is the busiest store in town. They have just opened for the first time since the war began. We hurry home after the long wait in line.

I can't stop thinking about the woman. I remember a story I read. It confirms that keeping silent was the wiser choice. It's about a Chabadnik who approached a passerby once. "Excuse me, did you lay tefillin today?"

The man refused the offered mitzvah and walked on. The Chabadnik watched as the man accepted the same offer from the next Chabadnik stationed some fifty yards away from him. His curiosity was so great, he asked the man as soon as he took off the tefillin, "Excuse me, sir. Can you please tell me why you refused when I offered you tefillin, and then accepted a few minutes later when my friend offered you tefillin?"

"Because when you offered me tefillin, I felt like you were doing it for your sake," the man said. "But when he offered me tefillin, I felt like he was doing it for my sake."

ぴ ぴ ぴ

I am still thinking about the woman when I daven *minchah*. I guess I know I have some *teshuvah* to do, because I choose to talk to Hashem about it in my *Shemoneh Esrei* prayer.

"Hashem, I had no right to talk to that woman on the street today. The truth is, if I would have talked to her, I would have done it for me. She would have had every right to be angry and insulted. OK, so it would have been in her best interests, too, but she didn't know that. And she wasn't likely to accept it coming from a *frum*-looking stranger in the middle of the street with sirens screaming and Katyushas flying. So why do I feel guilty? What's really bothering me?"

Hashem answers my almost inaudible whisper right away. I flash back to a scene at my school a few years ago.

෬ ෬ ෬

"You're going to call Mrs. Cohen and apologize immediately," I said firmly to Shirel.

"OK," the ninth grader said meekly, looking down at the floor.

"What got into you? My friend comes to our school. She volunteers her time so that you two girls can interview her for your English assignment, she pays for her own cab, and you wind up screaming at her at the top of your lungs? What was it all about anyway?"

I already knew. Mrs. Cohen had told Shirel her family didn't want their sons to serve in the army. Shirel felt differently, and she didn't have a long fuse.

"Morah, I'll call her. But you've got to understand something. This lady is the first *chareidi* person I have ever talked to in my whole life. I wasn't just yelling at her. I was yelling at all of you, everything that has been bottled inside for years."

"What about me? I'm more *chareidi* than anything else."

"You don't count. You're my teacher."

"Shirel, it isn't possible that she is the first. Tzefat is 50 percent religious, and the *chareidim* are a big part of that religious segment. We walk down the same streets together. We shop in the same stores. We wait at the same bus stops. We stand in the same lines at the supermarket. How can it be that she is the first *chareidi* you've ever talked to?"

"I don't know. She just is. This isn't the kind of thing you talk about to a stranger on the street."

The flashback ends.

Thank you, Hashem. Now I know what I have to do teshuvah for. I have to do teshuvah because I don't love that woman. I don't love her. Sobs. I don't love her. I just want her to change because she is endangering my world and delaying the geulah. Help me, Hashem. Help us all so that we are not like strangers passing on the street.

By the litmus test of the holy Tiferes Shlomo, the first Rebbe of Radomsk, it was a good davening. He wrote, "You know your *teshuvah* has been accepted before Hashem when you feel *simchah* after pouring out your broken, crushed heart."

Day 16

Date: July 28, 2006
From: Chana Besser
To: Tzefat under Fire list
Subject: Rabbi Leff on Elef L'Mateh, 1992

In 1992, at a shiur, Rabbi Zev Leff talked about when he was rosh yeshivah during a war in Israel. Rabbi Leff spoke about a certain passage that day. The Torah says the line twice: "A thousand per tribe, a thousand per tribe..." It doesn't mean two thousand men had to go to war from each tribe. The meaning of the repetition is that 1,000 men were to go forward on the battlefield, and 1,000 men from the same tribe were to study Torah, pray, say tehillim, and do extra deeds and mitzvos to protect the soldiers who were out there on the front lines.

I don't want to scare you with this, but Rav Leff — I'll never forget this — told his boys in yeshivah that day (as I remember it), "OK, our soldiers are in the trenches, in the tanks, out on the front line. And they don't get to go home and sleep in their cozy beds after a ten- or twelve-hour day. They are on duty and on call twenty-four hours around the clock. As of now, so are we. Yeshivah learning hours are extended (I don't remember exactly, but it was every waking hour).

"And I want every boy here to know that if he so much as stops learning Torah for two minutes to take a drink of water at the water fountain, for those two minutes, he is endangering a Jewish soldier's life on the battlefield."

Faith under Fire

CHANA BESSER

A Step Closer to Geulah

Sunday, July 30, 2006
5 Menachem Av 5766

E lisheva called to tell me this story. She just heard it on Israeli radio this morning:

There are two factories in Israel that are fierce competitors. Between them both, they have most of the market share. One factory is in Nahariya, and it had to close because of the missile attacks. It looked like the employees would have no work and no pay for the duration of the war.

Its competitor is located somewhere around Migdal HaEmek, a far less dangerous place, so it was open as usual. The owner of the open factory called his rival who had shut down.

"Listen, bring all your workers down here with you to my plant. I'll operate during the day shift, and you'll run your business here during the night shift."

We just took a giant step closer to the *geulah*! The angels must be doing somersaults up there in Heaven.

They say a Jew can be compared to an olive. An olive has wonderful, pure oil inside. But the only way to access it is to squeeze the olive. The true nature of every Jew — let me repeat: every Jew — is to be a giver. Wars bring out our love of one Jew for another, our deepest desire, which is to give.

Hashem loves His Jewish children. He protects us. It's that simple. He knows what is deep inside every Jew. He's just scaring us enough to bring out our innate goodness. Yes, the price is high. But the value is also dear. And don't forget, our Creator and Sustainer has His personal accounting with every one of His creatures. Nothing is random.

Personally, I'm praying for this war to be the last war. I'm praying for it to continue until every Jew in the world is flowing with giving like pure oil from an olive. We are suffering here too much — refugees in the center of the country, people in the North scared in homes and shelters, no money, businesses ruined — we are suffering too much for this to end as just one more war that doesn't solve anything. I'm pushing for the *geulah*.

Let's promise ourselves to stay close to G-d, to keep our hearts open, to do what we always knew was the right thing to do after life goes back to normal. It's a big promise, but without it, this war just isn't worth the price.

This essay was first published in *Hamodia* weekly newspaper.

Day 18

Date: July 30, 2006
From: Chana Besser
To: Tzefat under Fire list
Subject: I'm alive in Tzefat and Pam Waechter was killed in Seattle

I keep telling you people, it's safer for a Jew to be in Israel.

I'm alive in Tzefat, baruch Hashem, may He continue to protect me. And Pam Weachter was killed at the Jewish Federation in Seattle by a Muslim gunman on Friday.

Go figure. She was just going to work. So, everybody, please relax and just keep praying for me, for all the Jews in Tzefat, for our soldiers, for all the Jews in Israel — and for all the Jews outside of Israel just going to work in the morning.

Date: July 30, 2006
From: Simcha Layah
To: Chana Besser
Subject: We are safer in Tzefat

Hi Chana,

When this war broke out, my family was trying to get me to leave Israel, offering me plane tickets and a credit card. One brother offered me a house to stay in with my children, plus the use of a car — in Seattle. Imagine if that Arab terrorist had seen me walking the streets of Seattle with my boys with their kippot, peyot, and tzitzit? I

feel safest right here, at home in Tzefat!
Love,
Simcha Layah

Date: July 30, 2006
From: Chana Besser
To: Tzefat under Fire list
Subject: It's the Arizal's yahrtzeit today

It's the yahrtzeit of the Arizal today and there are around 50 people standing in the cemetery at his kever while this town is under missile attack! I stayed in my house and lit a candle for his neshamah to have an aliyah.

Some 40 rockets landed in northern Israel on Sunday morning, resulting in damage and wounding five people. I haven't heard of anyone being hurt in Tzefat, haven't heard any ambulances, just lots of booms, mostly distant this morning. Those of us still here are adjusting to life with constant missiles exploding and the sound of the armies launching bigger bombs over the border. I still can't tell too well which distant booms are big bombs in Lebanon or Katyushas striking closer towns like Meron or landing in the wadi — they sound the same to me.

During the Gulf War I was in America. I watched the nightly news reports about how the fancy US electronic system was saving so many lives. I didn't know the truth until I moved to Israel.

"Are you kidding?" they told me when I got here. "It wasn't the fancy technology that saved lives. It was miracles — out and out miracles. If they tell you it was the electronic defensive system, then how do they explain the fact that nobody was killed before they engaged it?"

America can stop working on their anti-missile technology. We don't need it. We have our own sophisticated, spiritual anti-missile protection. It's called TAMMCATT. It stands for Torah, achdus, mitzvos, middos, chesed, teshuvah, and tzedakah.

Day 19

Date: July 31, 2006
From: Ariella Bracha
To: Tzefat under Fire list
Subject: It was scary but I would not trade it for anything

Shalom, dear friends,

As some of you may know, we are in Tzefat helping out. We just experienced two of the most amazing days of our lives, experiences that will be embedded in the very fiber of our being…helping people and hugging them and giving smiles and so much more, but that is for later.

We had just finished giving away challot, candy, cakes, and Shabbat candles to very, very poor people that Hashem directed us to. We were driving when a rocket landed around 300 feet from our car. It rattled the ground and vibrated the car and I thought the windows were going to explode right in my face but, baruch Hashem, we are safe and home. Since we were in the car and had heard no warning siren, we didn't know what to do, so Avraham stepped on the gas. We are completely in awe of the chesed of Hashem in our life and for protecting us.

Yes, it was scary but I have to tell you honestly…I would not trade what we experienced the last two days for anything. We will stay and continue to help because we have stared fear in the face, the fear of coming up here to help. If my time came, chas v'shalom, I know that my relationships with family and friends are healthy and good. But just in case, please forgive anything I may have done intentionally to cause you pain or sadness. The most important thing, though, is that my husband and I are completely of one mind and heart. Sharing these times together side by side allows me to have a greater awareness of his inner light and beauty as I watch him give to others. I am so filled with joy and peace, baruch Hashem.

And now, we are going to take a nap in our safe room and then get ready for Shabbat and cook for guests...

Shabbat Shalom!

Love, Ariella Bracha

• • •

July 31

Subject: If your home was damaged — read this before you fix anything.

An important piece of news to share:

Call 106 and someone will come out to assess the damage and assign it a cost for fixing. THEN, individuals and homeowners should pay for the repairs and bring the receipt to this organization who will issue a check to pay for repairs.

So if you return home to discover windows blown in, do not pay to have it fixed before the assessment is made or you will not be reimbursed.

Moshe Chaim

Day 21

Date: August 2, 2006
From: Chana Besser
To: Tzefat under Fire list
Subject: Names of wounded soldiers for prayers

> Can anyone get an update on which of these soldiers should stay on the list for prayers?
>
> Among the wounded soldiers who should be mentioned in the prayers are the following five who were wounded in Lebanon on July 26:
>
> · Ariel ben Janette
>
> · Shaul ben Shulamit
>
> · Gal ben Shoshana
>
> · Yuval ben Yehudit
>
> · Guy Yosef ben Ela

Date: August 2, 2006
From: Chana Besser
To: Tzefat under Fire list
Subject: Anti-missile defense system, Tzefat style

> In Building Seven of Me'or Chaim, three little boys launched their own anti-missile defense system. Datya Cohen and a friend had gone down into their building's bomb shelter to entertain the kids. "Let's make toy rockets and fill them with mitzvos," her friend said.

So they took toilet paper rolls and covered them with aluminum foil and wool.

"Now write down all the mitzvos and chesed you will do from Tishah B'Av until Tu B'Av," they told the children, "and put the little scraps of paper in the slot on your rocket."

"Let's shoot our mitzvah rockets against the Katyushas," Mordechai Leib, six and a half, told his little brothers. And so with every siren they would open the windows on the safe side of their apartment and aim their toy rockets, pretending to fire them, in the direction of the booms.

"Did it help the children to be less afraid?" I asked.

"I think so," Datya said.

• • •

Money for Tzefat people in need

Hallelukah! The city of Tzefat finally has some money for needy families.

I am supposed to get a call from a social worker. I'm waiting. I've been waiting since last night. She wants to know who is in need of emergency funds. To apply for emergency funds TO-DAY, e-mail me.

— chana

DEBORAH MILLER

Lamentation

Thursday, August 3, 2006
Tishah B'Av 5766

How does the city that was full of people sit solitary? On Tishah B'Av Jews lament the destruction of the Temple in Jerusalem and the long night of exile. Tishah B'Av is a spiritual rock bottom, a black hole of divine abandonment in which the covenant between G-d and His people seems smashed beyond repair.

My eye, my eye runs down with water, cries the prophet Yirmeyahu, *because the Comforter who should revive my soul is far from me.* On Tishah B'Av, as Jews fast and read the Book of Lamentations, an iron wall separates the gift of heaven from the sight of earth.

How then is this annual day of mourning followed by seven "Sabbaths of Comfort," when the relationship between G-d and His people is evoked in the verse from the Song of Songs, "I am my Beloved's, and my Beloved is mine"? How does the absent G-d become the Beloved? How can we find G-d at all in a world of indescribable suffering?

Judaism responds by asking, "How can we not find G-d there?" Torah emerges from the Sinai wilderness, the Talmud from the pit of Babylonian exile. Iyov, afflicted and bereaved, hears G-d speak from the midst of a whirlwind. Adam, hiding in the Garden of Eden, hears G-d's voice in the depths of his own despair. Where are you? The hidden G-d calls to us with our words to Him, and a dialogue is opened. The iron wall is breached. We are comforted by the fact of revelation in a place of darkness, by a call, a cry, a whisper born of our recognition of the great distance between G-d and man.

The world of Tishah B'Av is a world of broken dreams, of devastation and despair. For the Jewish people, it is an abyss of unimaginable suffering and a reminder of the recurring threat of annihilation. Yet from the abyss, redemption comes. The Mashiach, say the Sages, must be born on Tishah B'Av, for there is no great light but that which comes from deepest darkness.

On Tishah B'Av we sit by rivers of blood and tears that flow from Babylon to Babi Yar. How can we sing G-d's song in an ocean of suffering? *If I forget you, O Jerusalem, may my right hand wither, may my tongue cleave to the roof of my mouth...* Our longing is our one true song, wrote the Rabbi of Piaseczna in 1942 in the Warsaw Ghetto. It is the song of songs, from a world beyond words, the song of faith after Auschwitz.

> DEBORAH MILLER lives in Melbourne and edited the English translation of *Eish Kodesh* (The Holy Fire) by the Piaseczner Rebbe. She was in Tzefat learning with us the day the war broke out.

Day 23

Date: August 4, 2006
From: Laurie Rappeport
To: Tzefat under Fire list
Subject: Want to get married? Volunteer in a war zone

The Livnot U'Lehibanot campus of the Livnot Israel Experience Programs, an outreach organization, served as one of Tzefat's volunteer headquarters during the war. Volunteers came from throughout Israel and from overseas. Livnot executed the city Social Work Department's responsibility to deliver meals and care for the 120 abandoned elderly and handicapped in their apartments. They cleared out, cleaned, and repaired bomb shelters, including plumbing and electricity. They drove through town under heavy missile attack to bring food and medication, took people to doctor appointments or dialysis, and sat with them during missile attacks. Then, after a full day of vital work, they visited the wounded soldiers in the Tzefat hospital.

Two shidduchim were made. One was the son of the founders of Livnot who was coordinating the volunteers until his own call-up to the reserves; the other was an army reservist who used the Livnot campus as his headquarters as he coordinated emergency bomb shelter repairs throughout the city. Both found their basherts among the volunteers.

SARAH YEHUDIT SCHNEIDER

Exploring the Question: How to Deal with Our Enemies

The Ba'al Shem Tov explains that since the entire cosmos is one single, universe-encompassing Adam, everyone, including our enemies, is carrying a piece of his soul and we a piece of theirs. This does not mean that all souls are identical. Rather, each nation occupies a certain layer of this cosmic Adam.

Our mystical writings teach that the Jewish layer is the inner soul core of this archetypal human being. And just as a soul permeates every cell of one's body, so does the soul of *knesset Yisrael* permeate every cell of creation. Consequently, no matter what is required for self-protection on a physical level (and this essay is not at all addressing those kinds of questions), we still have to find a spiritual attitude to accompany that action, which will "sweeten the judgments," because anything else (so says the Ba'al Shem Tov) will only make things worse for us.

Basically this means that we must pray for our enemies to do *teshuvah* and to be redeemed. That is the only solution that is really a "win," and, even more, a win-win. The Ba'al Shem Tov explains that it is not because this is the most noble option, but rather he arrives at this solution from a place of pure pragmatics.

Any other attitude will only make things worse.

He further explains that if our enemy is really in the category of Amalek, with no redeeming spark, then the sincere prayer for their *teshuvah* will actually cause their demise. Consequently, there is no way to lose with this practice.

A War Prayer

Inspired by teachings from the Komarna Rebbe

Let it be that every Jew, no matter where they stand, no matter what they face, let it be that they should see the light [meaning Hashem's light]. And let them integrate that light so deeply into their being, into their heart, bones, and cells, into their thought, speech, and deed, that they (and we together) should become the light [meaning the light unto the nations that is our truth and destiny]. And we should shine that light out into the world with such force and radiance that all the nations of the world, and particularly our enemies among them, should see the light, Hashem's light [meaning Hashem's light as it shines through the Jewish people], and their hearts should open, their lives should turn, they should repent and be redeemed.

SARAH YEHUDIT SCHNEIDER is the director of A Still Small Voice (www.amyisrael.co.il/smallvoice), a correspondence school in classic Jewish wisdom. She lives in Jerusalem's Old City. Sarah has written *Eating as Tikkun*, *Purim Bursts*, and *Kabbalistic Writings on the Nature of Masculine and Feminine*.

Day 25

Date: August 6, 2006
From: Noga
Subject: Sitting in a shelter or in a windowless hallway

Shalom dear family and friends,

This is kind of surreal. You see, I like shopping in Wal-Mart. Fun for me means a day in the mall. I once even went into Saks Fifth Avenue and walked around a bit. How did I get into this war-zone mess? What am I doing here? Can I leave? Yeah, I was told to get in touch with the embassy and they will send me back to Florida. Do I want to go? You bet I do. Just let me loose at the nearest K-Mart! Am I going to go? Nah, I guess my idealism hasn't rotted with age.

So I'm here and I sit in a shelter or in a windowless hallway. I hear the thudding of the falling enemy rockets. The sounds of the rattling of the windows and doors when the missile lands. The fire and smoke. We had some heavy shelling attacks during Shabbos. A missile fell in back of our house and lit up the trees. The smoke was suffocating. Breathing became a little difficult. I stood near the window watching the sky turn pink and purple with the sunset clouded with smoke. Another day ending in fury.

How long can this last? I am an American — born and bred — used to constant air conditioning, instant foods, well-ordered traffic, polite people (did I mention malls?)… Sitting in bomb shelters was not part of my long-range plans.

I want to tell you all that eons after our enemy disappears we will still be here. We'll just hang on tight for the ride. Thank you all for your prayers. Please continue to pray for all of our people.

With much love, Noga

P.S. I am including a letter written by my friend, Yehudit:

From Israel with love:

It is after the Sabbath here in Israel. The enemy doesn't respect our holy days, though the world expects us to respect theirs. Old story. We've quit buying it. The rockets fell regularly on Sabbath, some close to my home...

We are hearing that many Americans are upset at Israel's "over-aggressive" stance — in other words they are saying that we are bombing too much.

If the USA were attacked by a pit of scorpions and snakes, you would kill them off until none existed. That's what Israel is doing, and may we continue to do it and not fall into the short-sightedness of the nations.

After WW2 many American Jews were asked what they did to help our European Jews caught in the Nazi death net. The answer was pretty much "nothing." Don't let us down now. Be there for us. Be a support. The enemy will always be there waiting for us — in Israel or at the World Trade Center. Don't be swayed by the unbalanced view of the media. Stand strong for us. We will come through this in the end. The question is, will you be with us — your brothers?

Day 26

Date: August 7, 2006
From: Simcha Layah
To: Chana Besser
Subject: Safe in Tzefat

Hi Chana,

I'm getting so much pressure, especially from my father, to leave. OK, so he saw what happened in Seattle [the shooting in the Jewish Federation Building], so he understands now why I wouldn't go to the States.

Then he offered me an all-expense paid vacation for my children and me to his island resort in the Philippines. Tropical luxury! He's there right now. He didn't understand why I would decline. I told a friend about the offer, and my friend just sent this to me:

> Philippines Evacuates 35,000 People as Mayon Volcano May Erupt
>
> Aug. 7 (Bloomberg) — Philippines authorities are evacuating as many as 35,000 people around Mayon Volcano, a tourist attraction southeast of the capital, Manila, after "small explosions" occurred early today... Mayon is one of the country's 22 active volcanoes...

Maybe the Phillipines are more dangerous than here. Maybe Dad should seek shelter in Tzefat.

SHANA HOVSHA

Trip to the Shelters

Thursday, August 10, 2006
15 Menachem Av 5766

Early this morning I left Jerusalem with three friends and traveled up North. We have been successful in sending trucks filled with ready-cooked meals and other supplies to people living in bomb shelters for the past few weeks. I wanted to have another opportunity to go to the North and connect with the people myself. Today was day 29 of this war, and for the soldiers fighting and the residents crammed into small unventilated bomb shelters it feels like far longer than one month.

I had already heard the news that had been reported in the early hours of the morning. Fifteen reserve soldiers were killed in Lebanon yesterday. Twenty-four were injured, some of them seriously. My friends were hearing this news on the radio for the first time as we were exiting Jerusalem, and the tension in the car was palpable. It set the tone for much of what was to follow the rest of the day.

More than eighty rockets were fired into the city of Kiryat Shemona yesterday. Already at the entrance to the city, I could see evidence of far more destruction than I saw two and a half weeks ago. Kiryat Shemona is the city that has suffered the most building damage in this war, followed by Nahariya and then Tzefat. Having said that, it is very important to emphasize the miracles that continue to occur here daily. According to yesterday's army reports, more than 3,200 rockets have hit northern Israel since the start of this war and only 5 percent of them have hit buildings.

While we were in Kiryat Shemona, I got a call from a friend who was at Ben Gurion Airport to welcome friends who were making Aliyah today on the Nefesh B'Nefesh plane. Sitting in this boiling hot, stuffy bomb shelter, I felt incredibly comforted knowing that 243 Jews had just chosen to make Israel their home and that this war had not derailed their plans or their determination. I heard that despite the war not a single person cancelled.

I told the woman sitting next to me, and the news spread through the bomb shelter like wildfire. Everyone had something to say about it. Almost everyone was amazed that people were prepared to make Israel their home right now. One man said, "When this war is over and the next Nefesh B'Nefesh plane arrives, I will be at Ben Gurion Airport to welcome them."

 C   C   C

2:30 p.m.

Sirens sounded again all over the North. By then we were in Carmiel. A home in the Ma'alot area was damaged in a Katyusha rocket attack and rockets landed in Rosh HaNikra. Firefighters and firefighting planes were battling to control forest fires from rocket attacks in the Golan Heights and Upper Galilee areas. I want you to know that this is what is happening here every day. Every single day! You will not see this on BBC and CNN, but this is our reality.

The strength of *am Yisrael* is so clear to me. Since this war began, I have been inundated with calls and e-mails from people here in Israel and all over the world genuinely wanting to help. People have sent money, and others have brought packages to my apartment filled with toys, books, games, clothes, and toiletries. *Chesed* is our strength and so is *tefillah*. The attitude of the people living day after day, night after night, in these small bomb shelters with horrendous conditions is exceptional. Despite the incredible difficulties, they have faith in Hashem. Wherever we went yesterday, people openly shared their feelings and thoughts, and in place after place we heard people say they were willing to endure all that this war entails so long as the government allows the army to complete their job and does not give in to international pressure.

For me, one of the most moving events of my day was distributing food and supplies to a group of soldiers. These soldiers are all very young — nineteen, twenty years old. They told me how the religious among them put tefillin on the secular soldiers every morning, how the secular soldiers have learned *Tefillas HaDerech* by heart from their religious friends. What made me cry (for the umpteenth time today) was when they told me how they sing "*Ani Ma'amin*" as they march into Lebanon to face Hezbollah terrorists. I thanked them profusely and told them that because Hashem has given them this holy work to protect us we are able to remain here.

ভ   ভ   ভ

3:15 p.m.

We were still in Carmiel. I was on the phone with someone in Kiryat Shemona when the siren sounded again, and we had to cut the call short so that he could get into a bomb shelter. The bomb shelter we were in was shaking and children were screaming. My heart was pounding. It was very scary, and I kept thinking that with all the experience these people have gained in the past month, this is just not something you get used to. A few minutes later I heard that sirens were also sounding in Shlomi, Nahariya, and other northern cities.

ভ   ভ   ভ

4:00 p.m.

We arrived in Haifa, took a short break for *minchah*. About fifteen minutes later, literally seconds after I finished davening, warning sirens sounded in Haifa, Carmiel, Nahariya, Rosh HaNikra, and surrounding areas. Residents were told to take cover in bomb shelters and protected rooms. We piled into the closest bomb shelter, and a bunch of children were sitting nearest to the entrance playing cards. Seeing four new faces in their shelter, they asked us who we were. I sat down next to them, and they asked me to play with them. They shared with me how hard this past month has been and how helpless they feel about their own reality. We spoke about ways people can help themselves in difficult times, and when I suggested that we recite *tehillim* together they were very skeptical. They spoke among themselves, and one of them told me very matter-of-factly that they would say "just one." Forty minutes later, as we said goodbye, these kids were still reciting *tehillim*.

❧ ❧ ❧

5:00 p.m.

In all the places that we went today, I was very aware of the large number of trees that have been destroyed by forest fires started by rockets in addition to the houses and structures. At approximately 6:15 p.m. three rockets were fired into Acco, and sirens were again sounded in Kiryat Shemona and surrounding areas.

❧ ❧ ❧

Throughout the day, I saw many familiar faces, people I had seen and met the last time I was in the North. One of the most heartwarming reunions was with my "Sudoku buddies" in Haifa. They showed me the Sudoku puzzle books I had sent them and told me they would soon be needing new ones.

I am very grateful to those of you who don't know me but were forwarded my first article and made the effort to call and e-mail me. To all of you who have generously contributed to my project, I thank you from the bottom of my heart! The money has allowed us to continue sending prepared meals up to the North daily, and I can tell you that the expressions on the faces of the people in the bomb shelters, especially the children, when we distributed the toys, games, clothes and toiletries was priceless. Thank you, thank you, thank you!!! May Hashem bless you and bless us to continue our work. Shabbat is coming in soon so I will have to end now.

SHANA HOVSHA made aliyah in 1994 from Johannesburg, South Africa, and lives in Jerusalem. She is a special education teacher and is known for her political activist work in Israel.

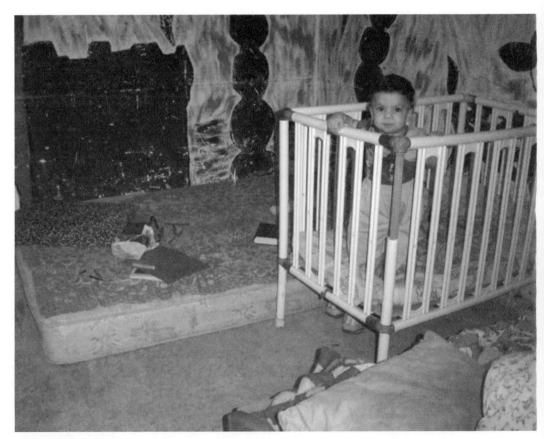

Life in a bomb shelter

Day 29

Date: August 10, 2006
From: Larry Rich, Afula, Israel's Emek Medical Center (EMC) Affiliated with the Rappaport Faculty of Medicine, Technion, Haifa, Israel
Subject: Our people, and our enemies

It's not easy to be an Israeli these days...or any day for that matter. The news reports of our brothers, fathers, children, friends, relatives, and associates who are fighting and falling in Lebanon have enveloped our lives in a choking black cloud of negativity. I cannot find a face that does not radiate the pain and foreboding that we are all experiencing. What more can I do other than share with you some of the conversations I've had this day?...

With Shira, a wonderful woman who occupies the office directly across the hall, opposite my own, and whose son is now commanding a paratroop unit deep inside Lebanon:

"Any word from your son?"

A grimace and pained body language before she answered, "No contact...nothing. It hurts me to say this, but I wish he would break his leg or be lightly injured in some other way so he could be brought home...to be near me."

The pain and fear radiating from her was unbearable. What could I say to her? That things would be all right? Not to worry?

With our CEO, whose youngest son is currently serving in the IDF and daughter and other son have received Tzav 8 (emergency call-up orders). I walked into her office and asked about her children.

For a couple of frozen seconds we looked at each other in silence before she answered, "I hope they're OK." A shrug of her shoulders and momentary raising of the eyebrows...gestures expressing the fact that their fate is in hands other than their own.

A phone call to Nama, who works in the local Jewish Agency office and who has brought many important visitors to our hospital. She has an eight-month-old baby, and her husband was called up via Tzav 8 yesterday. He's a medic serving with a tank unit. Armored units are being hit hard with advanced Iranian weaponry and suffering many casualties. She couldn't even complete one sentence without breaking down. Again...what could I say?

A phone conversation with the regional manager of our local Jewish Agency office:

"How are you and your family doing these days in Haifa?"

"Not very good. Sixty missiles have hit the city and many have fallen so near our home."

"Do you have a security room in your apartment?"

"No, only a communal bomb shelter for the building. We actually have to walk up fifteen stairs to get to it as our building is on a hillside." He lives on Mount Carmel in Haifa.

"Do you have time to get there?" Rockets travel quickly from Lebanon to Haifa.

"Not really. If we're dressed and ready to go, we can make it in about 20 to 25 seconds. For many alerts, my son, wife, and I just crowd into our three-foot-wide clothes closet and wait it out. It's the only place in our home not exposed to any windows."

A lady who volunteers in our ER walked into my office. She looked dazed and devastated. She stared blankly ahead and said, "Our next door neighbor's 26-year-old son was killed in Lebanon yesterday. My daughter was just beginning to deliver invitations to her upcoming wedding...and now all she can do is cry."

The window in my office faces the foot ramp that leads people from the parking lot to our hospital entrance. I was watching a family of four a short while ago when they suddenly froze and then began running towards the entrance. Air raid sirens! All of us quickly exited our rooms and stood in the long narrow hallway that has eight offices on either side facing one another.

The aimless chatter began. Blood drained from faces as people nervously shuffled their feet while trying to look comfortable. We waited. Would it be a muffled boom — meaning a hit several miles away — or a deafening thunderclap that would shake the foundations on which we stood and disrupt the very air we breathe?

Please allow me to set the records straight with regard to one central issue of this war. Hezbollah schmezbollah! Israel is at war with Iran. The aggressive army that is treacherously entrenched in Lebanon is Iranian born, trained, maintained, and supplied. They are not militia. They are not any paramilitary group. They are highly trained Iranian soldiers, indoctrinated with fundamentalist Iranian blood lust and executing Iranian intentions and policy. Iran, via impotent Syria, has dug the bunkers and poured the concrete into the heart of Lebanon. So please...let's at least get the name of the game right. Israel is at war with Iran.

• • •

Unprecedented Global Campaign Launched by Nefesh B'Nefesh to Bring 800 New Citizens to Israel Within Week

(NEW YORK) More than 800 North American and British Jews will move to Israel in the coming week as part of a six-day global aliyah campaign by Nefesh B'Nefesh, in close cooperation with the Jewish Agency for Israel. The first of four specially chartered El-Al flights departed New York's JFK airport, Wednesday, August 9. Three additional flights, from the U.S., Canada, and UK will land simultaneously in Israel next week, Wednesday, August 16th, resulting in record-setting Western immigration...

In total, more than 3,000 North American and British Jews are expected to immigrate to Israel this summer, on seven specially-chartered flights, through Nefesh B'Nefesh, an organization dedicated to revitalizing North American immigration to Israel.

"In the midst of these trying times...our four flights of new Israeli citizens over the next six days symbolize continued hope and optimism for the Jewish people," said Rabbi Yehoshua Fass, co-founder and executive director of Nefesh B'Nefesh. "Today's olim are no longer mere observers of Israel's modern history. They are creating it."

Since 2002, Nefesh B'Nefesh has been instrumental in bringing over 7,000 North Americans Jews to Israel. This is the organization's 18th aliyah flight to date.

BRACHA ADINAH DENTON

We Are All Crying

Monday, August 14, 2006
19 Menachem Av 5766

I have seen several friends from home today. We are all crying. How much more can we take? I feel like I'm breaking into a million pieces.

What do we do? Where do we go? Do we empty our homes in Tzefat and move elsewhere and start over? Some have decided to just move. It is getting too intense living without a home.

School starts in two weeks. People are out of money, out of time in the places where they are staying, feeling like life as they know it is totally collapsing.

What should we all do?

Hashem, please help us. Please show us what and where and how. Please, Hashem, give us the strength to get through this... We are getting very weak and we want to be strong. We know this is from You, but we are confused...confused... When is it going to end? Please, Hashem, we know You will pull us through this. Please, help us to be strong.

TUVIA NATKIN

Tzfat, August 2006

Burning iron flesh roars.
Louder a thousand times.
The Katyusha sings.
Searing air. Explosion.
Shockwave. Heat.
Stand beside the wall you crouched by.
Brush your knees. Now walk.
A raven stares from a pole.
A cat yawns.
Music soars from this charred earth.
The walls of Exile are on fire.

Day 33

Date: August 14, 2006
From: Chana Besser
To: Tzefat under Fire list
Subject: Cease-fire!

The enemy woke us up especially early today with dozens and dozens of missiles, a regular fireworks show. That'll be a few less in their arsenal for after the cease-fire. No booms since 8 a.m. The quiet is strange. I'll have to work harder to feel Hashem's closeness now.

10:00 a.m.: there were long lines in the post office and the bank and lots of cars on the roads. These are the people who have stayed low in town, moving freely about for the first time in a month. We'd better get our shopping done before the rest of the town comes home.

12:30 in the afternoon: I hear the plastic wheels of the first piece of luggage scraping over the rough cobblestones. People are coming home!

chana

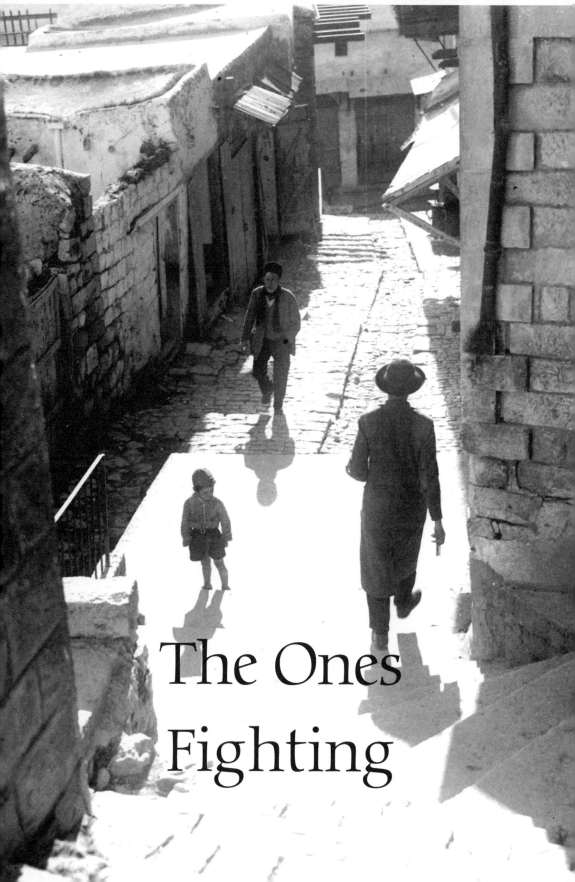

The Ones
Fighting

CHANA BESSER

First Tefillin

Malkiel Lerner knows his way around hospitals. Malkiel means "G-d is my King," but he likes to call himself "brother of the wounded." For eleven years he has visited terror victims and soldiers in hospitals all over Israel. This last war kept him busy. He lives in Jerusalem and traveled to the Rambam Hospital in Haifa every weekday for three weeks to visit soldiers wounded in Lebanon. Only seriously wounded soldiers are flown to Rambam. The lightly wounded spend a few days in the Tzefat Rivka Ziv Hospital and then go home.

One soldier in Rambam Hospital was so happy to be alive that he wanted to put on tefillin — for the first time. His family in Russia didn't know much about Judaism.

"Do you have tefillin?" the soldier's girlfriend asked Malkiel. It seemed like a reasonable question to ask a Jew with a *kippah* on his head.

"For what?"

"My boyfriend wants to pray and thank G-d for keeping him alive."

"It so happens," Malkiel relates, "I had my tefillin with me."

"Ask if he is a leftie or a rightie."

"He's a leftie."

"As if 'by chance,' I am also a leftie, so my tefillin were suitable for him."

Dan Brock bringing watermelon to soldiers on the front line

Miles with soldiers on the front line (see p. 196)

"Does your boyfriend have a *kippah*?"

"No."

Malkiel took a paper napkin, clipped it onto his head with *kippah* clips, and gave his own *kippah* to the soldier to wear. He put the tefillin on the soldier and said the *berachos* for him, but only the girlfriend said amen.

"He can't hear since the blast," she told Malkiel. So he wrote out the prayers *"Shema Yisrael,"* *"Baruch Shem,"* and the *shehecheyanu berachah* in full for the soldier to read.

"His girlfriend cried and I had goosebumps," Malkiel remembers.

ALIDA AND MILES BUNDER

On the Border

B oaz was sitting in his armored personnel carrier on a swivel chair with six computer screens in front of him, directing the firing of sixty shells from his company of 165 mm mobile cannons. When he finished, he turned around and said in perfect English: "Alida and Miles, so good to see you."

 C8   C8   C8

Last Thursday, Doron, whom you might see on CBS and CNN as an IDF spokesman, called us and asked for our help. He travels to every base in Israel on the Lebanese border. There is one artillery base that no one gets to because it is so well hidden. We asked if we could collect stuff and bring it to the soldiers based there. Doron first had to clear the way for us to go.

So Friday Rena got her friends together from Mitzpeh Nevo (one of Maaleh Adumim's religious neighborhoods) and sat outside the supermarket, and Alida did the same at the Maaleh Adumim Mall. Before Shabbat they had filled our station wagon with snacks, toys, and games. We then used the money and supplies sent to us and added to the already crowded car: two hundred T-shirts, a hundred pairs of dark socks (so they don't reflect light in the night), a hundred mini-books of *Tehillim*, electric water heaters, coffee, sugar, a hundred hats, CD players, and soap and shampoo.

Sunday morning we took off for the North. Upon reaching Lake Kinneret, we entered a surreal ghost town. We passed through Tiberias seeing not one car, not one person, not one store open, umbrellas and chairs neatly set up all along the beaches and not a single soul in sight. All of our favorite places in the North — Tzefat, Rosh Pina, Lake Kinneret — empty. All of our favorite restaurants and coffee shops closed. The kosher Chinese restaurant had been directly hit.

We can't tell you where we went, but when we turned down the final dirt road, there was a mobile artillery piece in front of us and one in back of us and a bunch of APCs in our little caravan.

Nobody stopped us. Nobody asked us where we were going. We just followed the instructions Doron gave us, and all of a sudden we heard the earsplitting sound of cannons. As we looked down into the valley, we saw a bunch of artillery, flashes of light, and, a second later, the sound of the blasts and the whooshing of the shells as they soared just above our heads.

As we neared the command post, one of the soldiers suggested we open our windows or they would implode from the concussion of the blast. Magically, the shooting stopped, and Boaz was sitting in his armored personnel carrier on a swivel chair with six computer screens in front of him, directing the firing of sixty shells from his company of mobile 165 mm cannons. When he finished, he turned around and said in perfect English: "Alida and Miles, so good to see you."

We had never met him, but Doron had called ahead. We told him what we had brought, and tears came to his eyes. Boaz could have been twenty-five years old. He was the captain of a hundred young men. His grandparents are American so he spoke English fluently. When we asked where we could put the stuff we brought, he apologized and said he had to get back in the APC.

We asked, "What can we bring you next time?"

He said, "Beach umbrellas and underwear," and reentered his command vehicle.

We drove over to the tent area where a bunch of soldiers had been asked to unload the car. They were amazed at the quantity of

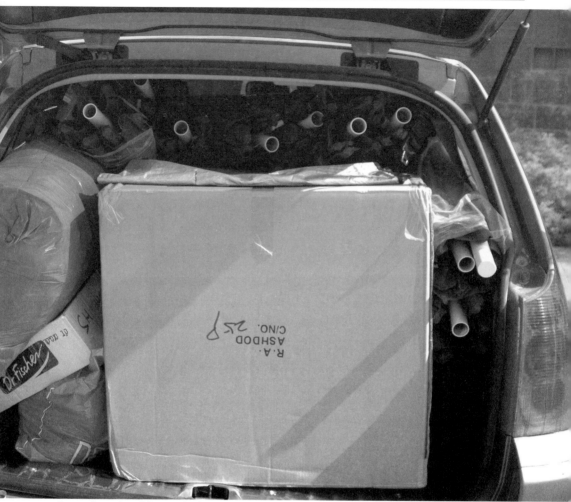

Care packages for soldiers on the front line

stuff we had brought for them. We asked what else they needed if we came back. Their answer was, "Nothing. We have all we need here."

Outdoor showers, Porta-toilets, tents open to the sound of twenty-four-hours-a-day shelling. The temperature registered 106 degrees with no trees. And all they could respond was, "Nothing."

We took some pictures and skedaddled out of there.

Our next stop was Yishuv Alma, a religious community of fifty families with an overview of the site in Lebanon with the worst fighting against Hezbollah. All the families are still there. We passed a bomb shelter with four children playing in its entrance, not willing to venture more than a few feet from the door.

We met Reuven, representative of the group, and gave him a huge box and six bags of toys and games. His children sleep with fear on their faces, not knowing which blast is from our side or theirs. They tiptoe outside in the morning afraid of what they will find. Did they appreciate our gifts? It was Chanukah all over for them.

Remember, these terrorists missiles have invaded our country. They have lobbed 2,000 missiles indiscriminately into unprotected houses, hospitals, factories, and stores. Today, two more people were killed in Haifa, and six more injured, one seriously. They are killing our people. Israel is at war. All over the North we saw Israeli flags on houses and cars, reminding us of Israel's Independence Day all over again. We saw signs proclaiming: WE WILL WIN! Other signs said: ISRAEL IS STRONG! We are a strong people, us here and you there.

May G-d bless the work of your hands, and may we see peace in Israel one day soon.

ALIDA AND MILES P. BUNDER are retired Jewish educators from Miami Beach, now living in Maaleh Adumim, Israel. After the war, they founded a nonprofit organization, Yashar LaChayal (Straight to the Soldier) www.yasharlachayal.org.il.

RABBI AVRAHAM BERKOWITZ

"Thank You for Your Protection"

This morning, as the sun rose over Jerusalem, my wife, Leah, gave birth to a beautiful baby girl at Hadassah Hospiital. A few hours later I drove to the southern Israeli city of Kiryat Malachi where my wife's parents live.

After packing several personal items my wife would need for her hospital stay, I set out to drive back to Jerusalem. When I passed the central bus station in Kiryat Malachi, I saw an Israeli soldier waiting to get a ride. I rolled down the window and asked him where he needed to go. He said his base was near Jericho, but if I could take him to Jerusalem that would be a great help.

I was in a particularly upbeat mood — after all, we had been blessed with our fourth child and third daughter — but the reality around me was worrisome. Israel was being attacked by its neighbors, and we were fighting a war to defend ourselves.

As fighter jets from the nearby air force base roared overhead, we cruised down the highway, and I got acquainted with Shachaf of Beersheva. His story gives a face to and direct association with the soldiers fighting for our land and people today.

Shachaf, twenty-one years old, was a medic in the IDF. He told me that yesterday his senior officer sent him home for one night to spend with his family because today he and his unit would be leaving their base near Jericho and heading up north to the battlefield on the border of Lebanon. They would be part of a team of doctors and medics who would be giving critical first aid to the wounded soldiers and civilians. His officer said he would not have any weekend breaks for a while and therefore sent him to bid farewell to his family. Shachaf told me of the feeling in his house that night.

"No one slept. They surrounded me with love and care. My father immigrated to Israel from Portugal in the late sixties and fought in the Yom Kippur War. My mother came from Tunisia to the promised land around the same time. They spoke of their dreams for themselves and our future.

"I am the third of four children and currently the only son in the army. My parents named me Shachaf, which means 'seagull' in Hebrew, but this morning when my mother said goodbye she held me for a long time and was crying. She kept calling me Rachamim, the Jewish name they gave me at my brit ceremony, which in Hebrew means 'mercy' and 'compassion.'

"She cried and said, 'Rachamim, today you will need G-d's compassion and protection. We all need G-d's *rachamim*.' "

As I drove, I tried to reassure Shachaf and spoke to him about the great role he had in protecting the Land of Israel and the Jewish people in Israel and, ultimately, Jews all over the world.

At twelve o'clock, I turned on the radio to the news. "Eight troops from Golani's 51st Battalion," the announcer said, "lost their lives on Wednesday during heavy fighting with Hezbollah terrorists..."

Shachaf asked me to turn off the radio and give him spiritual inspiration instead before he headed to the front lines. I shared with him thoughts that I heard and learned from my Rebbe and teacher, Rabbi Menachem Mendel Schneerson. During past conflicts in the Land of Israel, and during times of danger for the Jewish people, the Rebbe made practical suggestions of good deeds, mitzvos, that would elicit G-d's blessings and protection. I quoted *pesukim* from the Torah that speak of G-d protecting the land, and we discussed the need for us to understand the deeper truths as to why we have our permanent homeland specifically in Israel, as promised to us in the Torah.

Shachaf was very grateful to hear how Jews and non-Jews all over the world are praying for the soldiers fighting, thinking of them every day, and wishing for their success and G-d's protection.

When we came to Jerusalem, I opened my briefcase and pulled out a new mezuzah in a plastic case. I gave it to Shachaf and told him, "I am giving this to you for protection, but you must return it to me when you come back, and I will go to Beersheva and put it up in your bedroom."

Shachaf liked the idea. I said, "It says in the Torah, 'Emissaries of good deeds are not harmed.' You have a mezuzah — it will protect you." Shachaf put the mezuzah in his front left pocket and promised me he would leave it there until he returned. He said he would tell the story of our meeting to his fellow soldiers and tell them they had added protection.

We had only met an hour before, but suddenly we were deeply connected to each other. We embraced, the mezuzah protruding from his pocket and his rifle strapped across his chest. I looked at him with tears in my eyes and said, "Rachamim, thank you for your protection." He looked me back in the eye while placing his hand over the mezuzah I gave him and said, "Avraham, thank you for your protection."

RABBI AVRAHAM BERKOWITZ is the executive director of the Federation of Jewish Communities of the CIS, serving over 450 Jewish communities in the former Soviet union. He also runs a Chabad center in Moscow with his wife, Leah, where they live with their four children. He can be reached at berkowitz@jewish.ru. This essay was first published by www.chabad.org.

SUE TOURKIN-KOMET

Noam

The son of dear friends of mine, a *yeshivah bachur* and soldier, Noam Mayerson, *z"l*, of Jerusalem, was killed in the war in Lebanon a few days ago. His life and his death were a *kiddush Hashem* — a sanctification of the Name of G-d.

Noam was the epitome of a religious Jewish soldier. He had been a *hesder* soldier (a five-year program that combines religious studies with army service) and a *"tankist"* — a tank commander — and he had just finished his military service.

Noam was engaged to be married. The wedding invitations had already been printed, and preparations were moving full steam ahead — all for a wedding that will never be, a marriage that will never be, a family that will never be born.

"How long did he serve in Lebanon?" one might ask. The answer: six hours. He was killed in a major battle just six hours into being a combat soldier. This was Noam's very first call to reserve duty. His first and last battle. He was a young leader who gave spiritual pep talks to his fellow soldiers before entering the battle. He had just given a *devar Torah* regarding the justness of this war and that when going into battle, a soldier must not think about his loved ones and must concentrate on the job that needs to be done: protecting *am Yisrael*.

I attended the funeral late at night in dark, dead silence. We were about 6,000 people standing together in the Jerusalem

Mount Herzl Military Cemetery, one of the largest funerals ever held there for a fallen soldier. Noam is buried in a row of fresh graves, next to the other Jewish soldiers killed shortly before him.

At the funeral, time and time again the speakers spoke of Noam's eternal smile, his devotion to Torah learning, his inspiration and profound good example toward younger *yeshivah bachurim* in the yeshivahs of Eilat and Mitzpeh Ramon in the Negev.

At the *shivah*, his mother tearfully said, again and again, "We hadn't even had time to begin worrying about Noam. We hadn't had time to absorb that he was in Lebanon. Only six hours had gone by, and then the dreaded team of military officials came to our home to tell us... When you have three sons serving in the IDF and your doorbell rings and you open it to see three uniformed officers, you know that the message you never wanted to hear has come to your doorstep. Our only question was 'Which son?' "

My heart is broken for his fiancée, his parents, his siblings, his elderly grandfather in Ohio, all his relatives, all of the yeshivah students and soldiers for whom he set a profound example, and for his never-to-be-born progeny. I ache in my heart and in my soul.

SUE TOURKIN-KOMET, originally from Washington, D.C., made aliyah to Jerusalem in 1968. Published in some thirty publications worldwide, in 2005 Sue received a Writer's Grant from the Office of the President of Israel for publishing her first book.

RONI KADISH

Unaware

The smell of peppermint so pungent
I want to taste
leaves crushed underfoot.
Green daffodil swords
battle with gladioli in my garden.
My neighbor dozes,
an old cap shades his eyes.
He doesn't see the raven, open-beaked,
snatch an apple from the ground.
He doesn't smell oranges or lemons
or hear the bluebirds.
He doesn't see soldiers
walking to his door,
officer first,
doctor second.
What men come on a summer day
to jar a man from his sleep?

RONI KADISH was born in Boston, married an Israeli, and made aliyah in 1960. She has had poems published in Israel, Canada, and the United States.

LEIAH ELBAUM

Tishah B'Av in Her Voice

My sister answered the phone Tuesday night with Tisha B'Av in her voice. She had just gotten word that a friend was critically hurt in the fighting in Lebanon.

I had heard the news that night. They were reporting soldiers lightly wounded and moderately wounded, no one critically wounded. Sometimes they say "critically wounded" to break it to the family gently. Sometimes it means critically wounded; sometimes it means dead. My instincts told me it was the latter. With a deep sense of foreboding, I prayed that it was the former.

When I SMSed her a few hours later to see how she was doing, her reply was a curt, chilling two words: *Hu neherag*. He was killed. Taking in the newspaper Wednesday morning, the glaring headline mentioned the name of only one of Tuesday's three casualties, an uncommon name from a moshav close to Modi'in. With a sinking heart, I realized without a doubt we knew this family, too.

The phone rang again. This time it was my husband with Tishah B'Av in his voice. "Have you heard the news? Did you hear the names of the soldiers?"

One of the fallen, Yehonatan Einhorn, was the son of a man my husband sings with in a local chazzanut choir. Wednesday found us packed in among hundreds of mourners pouring into Jerusalem's Mount Herzl military cemetery. A calm, somber crowd quietly escorted the twenty-two-year-old paratrooper on his final journey. We arrived just as the military hearse did. To the chanting of a psalm, a group of young paratroopers lifted the coffin draped in the Israeli flag and made their way up the stone stairs, followed by an honor guard and more soldiers, many straight from the front. The throng of mourners fell in behind while a posse of media cameramen pursued the best shots of raw grief.

The area around the open grave was cordoned off to provide the immediate family and honor guard room to breathe. Nearby, wreath- and pebble-covered mounds marked the fresh graves of other soldiers killed during the current Lebanon war.

People continued to file in as the earth was filled in over the coffin and the bereaved father uttered the Mourner's Kaddish in a voice cracking with emotion. My husband was visibly shaken. "It's hard to see such a cheerful man so broken," he said to me through tear-bleared eyes. "He always has a ready smile, an optimistic word. It's agony to see this happen to such a man."

It was disconcerting, especially in Israel, to see such a large crowd standing so quietly. Even the crying was muted, restrained, without dramatic outpourings of anguish. The pain was clearly etched on the mourners' faces, but most seemed to bear it with a dignified resilience. The birds, too, were silent, despite the ample trees. Only the sporadic wail of ambulance sirens from nearby Shaare Zedek Hospital broke the stillness.

The scattered trees were insufficient to shade the multitude from the harsh midafternoon sun. An intermittent Jerusalem breeze brought some relief from the stifling heat, bringing with it the refreshing scent of native pine trees and rosemary bushes.

A few soldiers handed out bottles of iced mineral water from an industrial-sized cooler, but the supply was woefully inadequate, and people passed each bottle around, taking a sip, briefly placing it on their forehead and passing it on to whoever looked like they needed it most.

Eulogies were given by family members, by his commander, by rabbis who taught him, and by people from his village. The pervading theme was Yehonatan's great humility, piety, and devotion to Israel and the Jewish people.

Many of the speakers pleaded with the government to make sure that this time the army should be allowed to do their job, that Israel fight the enemy until it is no longer a threat, not to leave it strong enough to regroup and start this whole terrible war all over again in another few months or years. Our soldiers must not have died in vain.

The parents remain fixed in my mind — two sweet, humble religious Jews bravely meeting the most terrible of all with acceptance, faith, and understanding. They spoke with such warmth and love, and no bitterness, only determination that their son died doing what was right to defend his country fighting for its life, doing what he believed in.

The father spoke last of all, with words of such power and courage that I cannot even try to convey them. Yehonatan literally means "G-d gave" — he thanked G-d for giving him his son for twenty-two joyous years. He ended with a plea: *Dai* — enough, G-d. Please end the constant attacks on our country.

೫   ೫   ೫

The next afternoon, Tishah B'Av itself, I was back at Mount Herzl, this time to pay respects to my sister's friend, Michael Levin, an American immigrant killed in the same battle. As on Wednesday, the mourners included soldiers wounded in Lebanon and others who had come from the front, a sea of red paratroopers' berets peppered with the colors of other units. There were also groups of English-speaking youth visiting Israel on summer programs. They had been brought to the funeral to learn about the Zionist ethos and to gain an insight into Israeli life. A group of them entering behind me didn't even seem to know whose funeral they were attending.

"So who is this dead soldier?" one asked his companion.

"An American immigrant from Philly, I think."

"Really? An American in the Israeli army?"

"Yeah, it's going to be a military funeral. I hear they shoot guns and stuff."

As I was leaving, a counselor was addressing a British group, trying to convey to his charges all that this young soldier embodied in his life and death — self-sacrifice, devotion to his cause, idealism, and the courage to pay the ultimate price if that is what the defense of Israel requires.

Some of these wide-eyed kids from abroad were clearly overwhelmed by the whole experience. Others brushed off the heavy emotion of the occasion with glib jokes and bravado. The eulogies were briefer, simpler, than at yesterday's funeral, but they were no less moving or heartbreaking. They painted the portrait of yet another special, dedicated young man whose abundant promise had been cruelly and abruptly cut short, a man who crossed thousands of miles to fulfill his childhood dream of living in Israel and defending his people by serving in the elite IDF paratroopers.

His commanders spoke movingly, one reciting a poem he had written in beautiful literary Hebrew in memory of the fallen soldier. Several of the Israeli speakers did their best to say a few words in English for the benefit of family and friends unable to understand Hebrew. Their heavily accented, mistake-riddled English did nothing to diminish the obvious sincerity and love in their words.

Long after the huge crowds had left, a knot of close friends, family, and comrades-in-arms clustered around the fresh grave, weeping, talking, and remembering. The press with their intrusive telephoto lenses stayed, too, hoping for a good snap of the bereaved, the fresh pain, sorrow, and shock on their youthful faces, bright eyes glazed with tears and disbelief. One girl commented to her friend how shocked some of the American family had been to see the media at the funeral. "Mike would have liked it, though," she responded. "He would have loved all the cool cameras."

Hard to believe that only about ten years separate me from them. As I hugged my sister at the graveside, I had no words of comfort for her. All I could do was be there. I was about her age when one of my classmates was killed in the previous Lebanon war. I knew how she felt, but there was no consolation in saying so. At the moment of loss, it feels as though no one else can possibly understand.

Standing beside Michael Levin's friends, the memories of that terrible day seemed as fresh now as they had been all those years ago. Time may bury the ache, but it is always just beneath the surface.

> LEIAH ELBAUM is a stay-at-home mom and freelance writer. She lives in Modi'in, Israel.

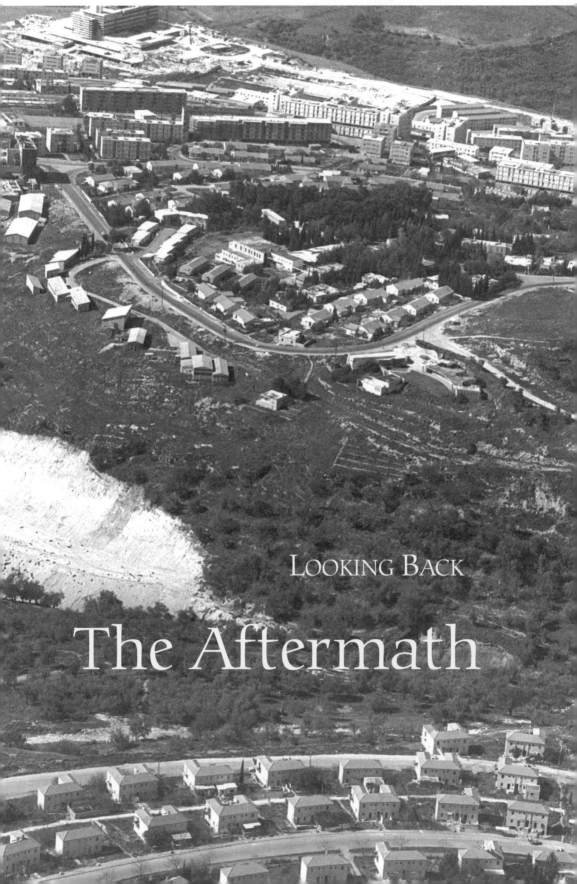

LOOKING BACK

The Aftermath

The Mor kitchen right after the rocket hit

Date: August 18, 2006
From: Chana Besser
To: Tzefat under Fire list
Subject: I'm going to the beach!

Early morning — second day of cease-fire and still quiet. People are starting to come home. Now we have to deal with the financial chaos.

It's 10:30 Friday morning now. We started to hear missiles exploding outside of Tzefat to the North around 10:00 a.m. Frume Goldberg called 106, and they explained that our army is blowing up the unfired Katyushas as they find them. (Good idea to explode them carefully without harm to anyone before we leave enemy territory.) So we can all continue with our Shabbos preparations, and all these tourists don't have to grab their Shabbos food and leave.

It seems to me that at least 70 to 80 percent of the town has come home. We have tons of tourists in town, not nearly as many as we usually have these three busiest vacation weeks, but, baruch Hashem, people are coming to their beloved Tzefat for their vacations.

I'm not going to access my e-mail for a few days. If there is something urgent, please call me. I'm going to the beach!

Blessings for a sweet and complete tikkun for our geulah, and a git Shabbos!

chana

WENDY TIKVA COHEN

Hope for Life

The Mor family turned Katyusha into kedushah. They are my neighbors and my friends. Here is their story, told directly to me over the past several months.

The Mor family was one of the first families to take a direct hit to their home on July 13, 2006, the seventeenth of Tammuz, as the fast day was ending. All the family was there; all miraculously survived.

Tzion Mor, thirty-nine, a quiet, introspective man, is a *sofer* of mezuzahs, tefillin, and Torah scrolls and an artist. Originally from Petach Tikva, he is of Iraqui and Greek ancestry. His wife Revital, almost thirty-five, beautiful inside and out, a lively mother of five precious children, is of Persian and Spanish ancestry and grew up in the same neighborhood as Tzion. She is an accomplished self-taught painter. Their children, Bat-Tzion (seven), Michal (six), Avraham Natan (five), Odel Chana (two), and Lia (one), will carry physical scars for the rest of their life. We pray the emotional damage will heal soon.

Later, Avraham Natan would tell his father, "Abba, you have no scars on you. You must be Superman!" Indeed, Tzion Mor's account of the events that evening, the evening their life would change, is one of a superhero.

"I had just left my family laughing and joking in the kitchen, to look for three stars on the balcony marking the end of the fast. Revital had finished cooking, and four of our children were in the kitchen standing near the refrigerator with her. I had only one foot on the balcony at the far end of the house, facing the hills of Meron and the *kever* of Rabbi Shimon bar Yochai, when it happened. I heard a loud whooshing sound and then *boom!* — an enormous explosion, an unbelievably strong 'force,' as Revital describes it.

"I ran toward the kitchen. The smoke was black and thick. It choked me so that I almost fell down and nearly passed out. It hits you in your throat, the smoke, like a burning knife. I waited a very short time, then entered what used to be the entry to the house and the kitchen. My eyes and throat were burning, but I had to go in and help my family.

"Through the dark, black smoke I began pulling out my children one by one from underneath the broken glass and fallen walls. The Katyusha had landed just a few centimeters from the doorway of the house. Revital was sitting less than a meter from where it landed. It blew a hole in a huge arch shape where the doorways and walls used to be. The two doors and part of the walls were gone, blown to pieces. I had to carefully lift each one of my children and almost jump across this huge hole.

"I remember thinking, *Where to put Bat-Tzion?* whom I picked up first, and then, when I went to get the others, *Where to put them all safely?* As I quickly leaped over the cratered hole with Bat-Tzion in my arms, I decided to place her against the far wall of the house adjoining us. Bat-Tzion's beautiful, sweet face was bleeding, and so were her back and other areas.

"Then I took Avraham Natan, also bleeding. The doctors say the metal shrapnel must stay in him for now. It's too dangerous to remove it. (Later he would have surgery on his abdomen).

"Then I picked up Michal, bleeding badly from her head, stomach, many places. Then Odel Chana. She was also bleeding, hurt in her head and in other places on her body."

"Each child was standing there with eyes wide open, with a look one would never forget. They were silent, dazed."

A nearby neighbor was standing on his rooftop and saw the Katyusha land. He ran with his teenage son to see if anyone was hurt.

The neighbor relates: "Two other neighbors, my son, and I came running and found four of the children outside their pulverized home covered in black soot. They had unforgettable bloody red pockmarks all over their little heads and bodies, bleeding from the steel bits and ball bearings that had been packed inside the Katyusha.

"The children were completely silent. They were in total, frozen, silent shock, just staring at one another, covered in blood and dust. The only sound was the gushing water from the water pipe that the missile had burst.

"We took the children down to the road. We stopped the first car and dashed them over to the hospital. We weren't even aware of the whereabouts of the parents. The children couldn't tell us anything, not even their names. Soon after we arrived at the hospital, the parents and another child came in, the mother seriously hurt."

One of the neighbors a month later was seen removing bits and pieces of shrapnel from a nearby tree, pieces like those inside the children. They were small, jagged, rusty metal.

While the neighbors were helping the children outside, Tzion was back inside the shattered house.

"I went back for Revital and told her, 'Come on, please get up.' But she told me, 'Tzion, I cannot get up. My leg, my leg!'

"Revital was amazing after the rocket hit. When I first entered the smoke-filled kitchen, she was still sitting on the chair, her hands stretched up to the heavens praying," said Tzion.

"I had to pray," Revital said. "When Tzion came into the kitchen, I was saying *tehillim*. 'Shir hama'alot — I will lift my eyes to the mountains. From where will my help come?...'

"I was aware of the explosion. I knew exactly what had happened, but at first, I wasn't sure if I was still in this world. I heard

The Mor family, healed and back home in their rebuilt house

my children crying, 'Ima, Ima,' before they went into shock, but I didn't know if I was hearing them from *Olam Hazeh* or *Olam Haba*. Then I realized that I was still alive, and immediately I knew that Hashem didn't want me to give up. I fought not to pass out. I knew I was hanging between life and death.

"What is Israel? A *chelek*, a part, of Hashem. He wants Israel to live. I had to do what I could to show Him that I wanted to live. I made my *hishtadlut*. I reached out to him. But it was Hashem who lifted up my arms. It was Hashem who was saying the *tehillim*, not me. He was right there with me, closer than ever before.

"I knew I had to stay awake. I wanted to pass out, but I knew I had to reach HaKadosh Baruch Hu with my prayers!"

Later they would discover that Revital had a crushed knee, a broken tibia, her fibula partially severed at the ankle, and many deep lacerations.

A neighbor came in when Tzion was trying to help Revital. He gently lifted the bottom of Revital's skirt and saw in horror the severity of the injury.

"I did not think I would keep my leg," Revital remembers.

Tzion continues, "Someone went to get bandages to secure her ankle before they could move her. Later, another next door neighbor — he and his family were miraculously saved from injuries by the horrible force of this Katyusha that blew their windows in on them — came rushing over. Three neighbors and I carried Revital out. Maybe someone else helped. I do not exactly remember."

Earlier Tzion had frantically searched for his baby, who was alone in the salon when it happened.

"After the four bigger children were outside, I began looking for signs of my baby, Lia. I could see very little because of the thick smoke and debris that was still everywhere. Then, suddenly, through the smoke, Revital and I saw something squirming and crawling toward us on the floor from the salon near the kitchen. I quickly realized it was Lia, scooped her up, and removed her from our mangled home.

"With Revital's leg now secured with bandages, we went down the hill through mud and debris to wait for the ambulance. At the local hospital, my children were put into different beds in the ER. They were crying, 'Ima! Abba!' I was running back and forth from bed to bed."

Revital remembers seeing Bat-Tzion's back in the ER. She was in the bed next to her. It was bleeding. "I remember thinking, *They know what evil is now. I could see in Bat-Tzion's eyes that she understood what had happened, what parents don't ever want their children to know.*"

Tzion remembers that Revital was in shock. "The doctors saw Michali's head and stomach injuries and said she needed to go quickly to Rambam Hospital in Haifa. I had to go with her in the helicopter. I had no choice.

"When we landed at Rambam Hospital, there were flashes of camera lights everywhere. I felt like I was some kind of movie star, only this was my daughter, badly injured! I put my hands up to cover my eyes from the bright lights. Just as they were separating us, I spoke to Michal. Then they quickly took Michal into surgery. She was in there for over five and a half hours for her head and her stomach. I could not believe this was happening. After the surgery they put her in a medically induced coma. The doctors said they would wake her up in a few days. That was late Thursday night. Before Shabbos she awoke. The doctors could not believe it. My Michal is strong, very strong!

"Revital's mother came to the Tzefat hospital, and my twin brother came from Tel Aviv to Rambam Hospital in Haifa. All I can say is 'Baruch Hashem!' Hashem made me leave the kitchen at that exact moment. Just half a minute after I left the kitchen the missile hit. Hashem had to remove me from there so I would be able to get my family out of that awful mess and be able to help my family now. We are all glad to be alive, loving and laughing, only two months later.

"My family, my mother, father, brother, sister, Revital's family, our friends and neighbors, everyone has been great. It is hard, running around all the time, taking everyone to the doctors for CT scans and waiting for their results, taking caring of their wounds, having Revital's cast changed (oh, that was so painful for her). It was hard going back and forth to Hadassah Hospital, over half an hour from Kibbutz Kfar Etzion, our wonderful host, where we were for nearly two months.

"Now my life is consumed with starting up a whole new house and taking Revital to the hospital, dealing with things not finished in the house and praying three times a day. Baruch Hashem, baruch Hashem! The children are a lot better. Revital will be in a cast for two more months (a total of four and a half months).

"How do I feel now? I can only say, 'Baruch Hashem!' "

ଷ ଷ ଷ

I had many conversations with Revital, some into the wee hours of the night. For a long time sleep was very difficult for Revital. The cast from her hip to her toes was only recently changed. It is now from her knee to her toes. And the pain — she seldoms speaks about it — is well hidden. She never complains.

Her leg is paining her now, I can see it on her face. I silently go over to her and do some energy work on her leg. Revital tells me it helps. She is so happy to feel more life in her leg. It is 3 a.m. She is finally able to sleep.

Another time we talk about Tzefat before the bombing.

Revital relates: "You know, one week before the war I went to Petach Tikva. As I walked through the bus looking for a seat, I remember seeing a woman davening *Shemoneh Esrei* sitting down. *I don't like this, sitting and praying. I won't pray sitting in chairs,* I thought. And now I must pray like this. Hashem wanted me to see this!

"I feel born again and yet sometimes feel like a heavy stone is on my heart. Everything I am doing is not real at times. I know I have so much more work to do. Everything is new — the *keilim* (kitchen utensils), the furniture — like we are just married and have to go out and buy everything new. But not everything inside me is new. This sense of starting over, it is not in my soul. I need to see it, absorb what is new, what I need to learn and know from this past experience. I need to understand and grow from it and stop wondering when I will be back home.

"I was so close to HaKadosh Baruch Hu at that moment when it all happened, when it seemed like I would leave this world. He was everywhere, filling me up completely with His goodness. I had to let go and know that He would take care of everything.

"When I realized I was alive, it was like a rebirth, a new awakening. I understand now the *teshuvah* I have done in the past. And it feels like I have to start this *teshuvah* all over again! Being so close with G-d makes you very aware of how much more you have to do in this world.

"Two and a half months later, I am beginning to feel lighter in my heart and in my head. Even my cast is beginning to feel lighter, though I cannot wait for it to be completely removed."

છ છ છ

Terrorists fire the Katyusha rockets on Israel. They are intentionally implanted with hundreds of pieces of rusty metal, nails, tacks, glass, steel ballbearings, materials injected with rat poison, and other cruel, inhumane, and physically damaging and painful substances.

The external scars may remain on the Mor family. They may scar their bodies for life, but not their souls. There are moments of aggression from the children, a release from the attack on them. Then I see these small children diligently cleaning and straightening up together quietly while both their parents briefly fall asleep from complete exhaustion. Tzion, their devoted father, awakes quickly with a dazed look, making sure his children are safe. They had hoped to be permanently in their home for Rosh HaShanah. It is not clear if that will happen. There is still much work to be finished on their home.

One time Tzion told me, "You know Revital — she is one with HaKadosh Baruch Hu."

"Yes, and so, I am sure, is Tzion one with HaKadosh Baruch Hu," I answered, admiring his unshakable faith.

We, the Jewish people, will always be one with each other and HaKadosh Baruch Hu. And no one, no missile, nothing can remove that connection from us, certainly not from the Mor family.

WENDY TIKVA COHEN is a practioner of traditional Chinese medicine, homeopathy, and nutrition. She founded Tikvah L'Chaim to help people of Tzefat and elsewhere who cannot afford alternative medicine.

A Letter of Thanks

To our dear fellow Jews, especially those who joined us in praying to Hashem for the safe deliverance of all of our fighters and refugees from the battlefront during the Three Weeks both in Lebanon and in northern Israel.

Please accept our outpouring of emotion at having seen over thirty thousand who prayed and accepted upon themselves to do more mitzvos for the sake of all of klal Yisrael and for specific individual souls of klal Yisrael. The spiritual faith and belief displayed by so many, both by those in need and by those who stepped forward and asked for divine assistance, not for themselves but for unknown others, was a rare and unusual display of solidarity that poured forth so freely from the neshamos of every Jew in klal Yisrael.

There is no way to convey the comfort and reassurance that those who live in the north of Israel felt when they knew people were praying for them. The same applies to the many soldiers who gained added confidence and strength knowing that unknown strangers cared enough to pray especially for them.

Thus we write this letter of thanks from the tens of thousands for whom you joined together to give spiritual assistance. We extend special thanks to the worldwide Jewish institutions who spread word of Project Elef LaMateh – Agudath Israel of America, the Orthodox Union, and the Young Israel. May their work on behalf of all of us enjoy continued success.

Although this chapter seems closed, let us continue to pray for the welfare of world Jewry and in particular for those who find themselves in harm's way, and especially those injured during this war and those three still in brutal uncivilized captivity, Gilad ben Aviva, Ohad ben Malka, and Eldad ben Tova.

With blessings from Zion for a healthy and peaceful new year,
Grand Rabbi Yitzchak HaLevi Horowitz, The Admor of Boston
Rabbi Simcha HaKohen Kook, The Chief Rabbi of Rechovot

Faith under Fire

CHANA BESSER

Who Says You Don't Get a Second Chance?

I look back on the four weeks I stayed in Tzefat amid sometimes over a hundred missile explosions a day. I remember my first cowardly thought the first Shabbos of the war, shortly after candle lighting, when the siren went off and the booms came close and heavy. *I should have left before Shabbos. This can really get bad.* And it did. Some of the explosions that night were within one or two blocks of my home. The belief that Hashem controlled where the missiles struck, and seeing them land in mostly open fields, courtyards, between homes, sometimes in empty homes, gave me the courage to stay. It wasn't until after the cease-fire that I remembered how strongly I had felt about Israel during the Six-Day War. Who says you don't get another chance?

My friend had walked up to me, tense and breathless. "Did you hear the news?" Whatever it was, it wasn't going to be good.

"No," I said. We were standing in the aisle in the middle of a lecture hall at the University of Illinois. Many other students were conversing in unusally somber, hushed tones.

"Israel has declared war," she said.

I was shocked. All of the groups of agitated students talking about the war were Jewish, I noticed now. None of us could sit down when the bell rang.

I don't think fast under stress. I couldn't leave the lecture hall. My friend left, and now I desperately needed to connect with another Jew, any Jew. So I walked all the way up the aisle to the high stage in the front of the lecture hall.

Dr. Weinstein, our funny, kind, chubby, middle-aged math instructor with a shiny bald head fringed with white hair, was standing in his usual spot, all the way to the left of the stage, way out in front. He was poised behind his trusty overhead projector as usual, his marker ready to write as soon as the students settled down. I always worried that he might trip on the extension cord, somersault over the projector, and fall off the stage, but he never did. He didn't know that Israel had declared war. I was sure of that. His body was relaxed, his gaze patient.

"Dr. Weinstein!" I had to scream to be heard above the din of three hundred students. He still couldn't hear me, so he squatted down on his heels to get closer to my voice. I stood on my tiptoes. Now there was only about a foot of space between my mouth and his ear. "Israel has declared war." It was me, a Jew, reaching out to be close to another Jew.

He tensed. His face betrayed his attempt to hide his concern. His eyes showed his shock and then, a moment later, his worry. "Class, please ask everyone who cannot hear me to be silent," he said into the microphone, controlled, calm, and experienced. "I have something to annouce that affects us all."

His tight muscles were the only clue that it wouldn't be about mathematics. A moment later, it was quiet. "I have been told that Israel has declared war. Anyone who feels they cannot concentrate is excused from this lecture. In five minutes, those of us who remain will continue our discussion of set theory."

Most of the Jews left, but I stayed. There was no suitable place on campus to be by myself and think. I didn't want to see the non-Jewish students laughing and socializing in the cafeteria or the student lounge, carrying on as if nothing had happened. I didn't want to take the subway and bus home to be alone in an empty house. So I just sat there. I had no idea what Dr. Weinstein taught. All I could think about was how much I wanted to jump on the next plane to Israel. I could pack a bag and be out of the house before my parents would get home from work. By the end of the lecture, I still hadn't made up my mind. It was crazy. I had never been further than Canada.

How's a twenty-year-old girl who still lives at home with her parents going to help Israel? I asked myself. I didn't even know how to buy an airline ticket.

"Thousands of students will go, that's for sure. It isn't crazy," my brave side tried to convince me. "It is the natural instinct of a Jew to worry about the survival of the Jewish nation. Israel is in danger. Of course I should go."

"Anne, you only know one word in Hebrew: *shalom*. You can't help if you can't communicate," my scared side argued. "You'll get in the way. They'll laugh at you. What's worse, you'll put others in danger. You don't have any skills they need."

It didn't take so long to convince myself that it would be OK if they sent me home. I would go anyway, my loyal side decided. I couldn't sit there, comfortable in Chicago, studying for tests and munching on Fritos while the ten o'clock news showed my people in danger and their national existence threatened.

It was good that the math lecture was a double period, because it took the whole first hour to dismiss all the irrational fears and excuses that the scared side of me offered. Only then did the real reason surface. How does a child of Holocaust survivors tell her orphaned, sole-surviving parents that she is flying into a war?

"Mommy, why didn't we go to Israel when we left Europe after the war?" I remembered asking when I was a child. "If the Nazis didn't kill me," she answered, "I wasn't going to give the Arabs a chance." I remembered how stiff and grim she looked when she said it.

Sitting in that lecture hall, I admitted that my life was not mine alone. Most of my family lay in unmarked, mass graves, or, worse, had been gassed and then cremated during that darkest of dark times before I was born. My sister and I were carrying a heavy burden. We two lone daughters had been born to honor the memories of hundreds, maybe thousands, of Bessers and Borzykowskis that had lived for centuries in Poland. I felt all those souls living through us.

It's very noble, but what right do I have to die? Who else do my parents have alive? I asked myself. I imagined their horror if they found out that I had gone. I tried to picture myself telling them that I was leaving for Israel. I couldn't conjure up the image. I knew I couldn't tell them. And if I couldn't tell them, then I certainly couldn't leave without telling them.

All night I thought about it, and then the next day and the next. Every hour I wanted to leave for Israel, and every hour I let my fear and guilt, as well as my sense of responsibility, convince me not to go. I went to school each day, but couldn't concentrate. All the while, my heart was with Israel, my ears on the alert for every news report. My brain and heart were arguing fiercely against one another, and I was very confused.

I never mentioned my agony or my fears to anyone. No one I knew left for Israel, but I heard amazing reports on the news of thousands of Jewish young people flying there to volunteer. How I wished I were one of them.

In six days Israel won the war. I was grateful to a G-d that I had prayed to for the first time in many years. I didn't really expect Him to answer my prayers because I had never paid much attention to Him before. But I prayed anyway, hoping that my meager words would somehow tag onto and go up with the more favored prayers of other, better Jews, like a faint echo.

The Six-Day War was over. I had made one of the biggest decisions in my life and already I regretted it.

ନ୍ଦ ନ୍ଦ ନ୍ଦ

I grew up and learned how to buy an airline ticket. I married, had children, divorced, raised my children, and traveled around the world. Somewhere along the way, I became a religious Jew. And I moved to Israel.

Every people love their land. Every people will fight and die for their homeland. But the Land of Israel and the souls of the people of Israel are connected in a very special way.

The first settlers came to America by accident. They were looking for India. They were hungry, they were prisoners, they were religiously persecuted. They were happy to live anywhere that might be better than where they had come from. So they stumbled across America and decided to stay. A few generations later, their descendants sing, "My country 'tis of thee, sweet land of liberty..." This is natural. Humanity instinctively loves its land and its country.

How much more so should a Jew be willing to live, and die, for Israel? The *Zohar* says Hashem designated the Land of Israel for the children of Israel before He created the universe. None other than the Creator of the universe gave this Holy Land to His Jewish children. He declared it our land, established it as an eternal covenant, and wrote it into His Torah for the whole world to know and to remember. Our Jewish souls derive our life force, are sustained, from our connection to the Land of Israel.

Our ancestors dreamed of Israel, yearned for Israel, spoke of Israel, risked their lives, traveled for years, just to take four steps on the holy soil of Israel. A religious Jew says "Israel" or "Jerusalem," or one of the many other names that allude to Israel, a hundred times a day in his prayers.

Up to the year before I was born, the British were shooting any Jew who tried to enter Israel. Now any Jew can hop on a plane and walk freely in our Holy Land. I should leave so fast? As if it were any other land? I am not living here just for myself. I am living here for all my ancestors who couldn't live here, for all the Jews who want to but cannot live here yet, and for all the Jews who are so lost that they don't even care to live here. Soon they will all come home, please G-d.

If I would have been caught in a war in any other country, I would have run for safety. I believe the great rabbis and kabbalists who have said repeatedly that Israel is the safest place for a Jew to be in this generation. In fact, I worry for Jews living outside of Israel.

I'll tell you the truth. I've always had a problem with being a little stubborn. There were two occasions during the war when I failed to use my stubbornness to serve Hashem. Both of them were *simchahs* that I should have left town to attend. The first was Eliyahu Heller's bar mitzvah in Jerusalem. To be frank, I was afraid that if I experienced a few days without shelling, I would lose my resolve and not come back. The second was a friend's wedding less than an hour from Tzefat. She had hired a minibus to bring her guests to the affair. I should have gone. I was afraid to be surrounded by glass on the open roads. My *emunah* is growing. It's not perfect. I didn't use my stubbornness wisely then. The forces of evil triumphed briefly.

After the cease-fire, people rushed up to Tzefat to view the Katyusha damage. Many asked me, "Why did you stay in Tzefat? It's a commandment to guard your soul very carefully. You could have traveled south to a safer city."

"If someone doesn't feel the protection of the Shechinah, then they must take every precaution to avoid danger. But there are those of us who worked on drawing closer to Our Creator and Sustainer, worked to feel the Shechinah envelop us. Do you think the enemy has the power to shoot a missile and hit me, *chas v'shalom*, without the consent of My Father in Heaven?"

SHIRA YEHUDIT DJLILMAND

Before the War

Before the war
they would ask the usual childish questions
You know:
"Ima, why is the sun yellow?"
"Can we fly there in a plane?"
now they ask me,
"Ima, why do the Arabs want to kill us?"

Before the war
they would sleep deeply, secure in their innocence
now they wake screaming
convinced there is an Arab in their room

Before the war
they would play freely, happy and independent
now they cling desperately to my hand
a blanket, a pacifier
hoping it will save them from the bombs

Before the war
they were children, unaware of evil
their innocence intact
but now it is
after the war
and they will never be the same

CHANA BESSER

Rescued by Kindness

Angels from Switzerland

Now that people are home, we're hearing their stories about what they went through while being homeless for a month. When it comes to kindness, one family won the lottery.

The Levis left Tzefat before the first Shabbos of the war. Their three young children were screaming with every siren and every missile explosion. There were four explosions very close to the house by the time they had left town. Like most of the people who left before the first Shabbos, they hoped it would be safe to come home after Shabbos and took very little with them.

They fled to Tiveria for Shabbos, but four missiles exploded there, one right over Mr. Levi's head. A week later, Netanya was their fourth city of flight, they had spent the last two nights in unbearable circumstances, and Mr. Levi was sitting in a coffee shop near the beach having a lousy cup of coffee. He was facing up to the reality that they would have to bring the family back to Tzefat and spend the rest of the war in a bomb shelter. It had to be better than the last two nights.

"Anything about Tzefat on the news?" he asked the café owner, who had a TV in the shop. The man ignored him.

"Excuse me, did I hear you say 'Tzefat'?" a woman asked him. She and her husband had just walked in from the beach.

"Yes."

"Are you from Tzefat?"

"Yes."

"How are you doing?" the woman's husband asked.

"I'm down to my last few hundred shekels."

"Is there anything you need?"

"Yeah, a valium."

"Don't worry," the husband said. "From this moment on we are going to take care of you until after the war, no matter how long it might last."

They were true to their word. A wealthy Jewish family visiting Israel from Switzerland, they apologized for not being able to invite the Levi family to share their Netanya vacation home. It was already full with their family, and the wife's parents were visiting, too. They paid for a hotel room overlooking the sea and arranged for two *mehadrin* catered meals a day. They invited the Levis for Shabbos meals. In the honor of their religious guests, the whole Shabbos was catered *mehadrin*. And no one would turn any lights on or off as long as the Levis were present.

The Swiss couple noticed that Mr. Levi wore the same clothes on Shabbos as he had worn on Friday when they had met him. Early Sunday morning, there was a knock on their hotel room door. They had bought toys and diapers and a whole wardrobe of new clothes. All the sizes were perfect. The hotel didn't offer laundry service, so the wife came by every two days, picked up their laundry, and brought it back clean for them.

"Is there anything else you need?" the husband asked.

"Tefillin. I left my tefillin in Tzefat. We only left for Shabbos."

They borrowed tefillin for him.

On Tishah B'Av, as soon as the fast ended, the Swiss couple was at their hotel room door with pizza and Ben and Jerry's ice cream.

They were doing the same thing for ten different families from the North. A week and a half before the cease-fire, they returned to their home in Switzerland. Before leaving Israel, they gave the Levi family nine hundred shekels and the keys to their Netanya apartment, fully stocked with food, new bottles of shampoo, and everything else they might need.

Mr. Levi was happy to bring his family home as soon as the cease-fire began. He looked at his almost empty wallet, thought about the bills that would be waiting for him, his business that had been closed for a month, and forced himself to make a vow. It wasn't much, but just to show his appreciation for how Hashem had sent him so much kindness from another Jew whom he didn't even know, he told himself he would give fifty shekels to the first soldier he saw in Tzefat.

"I don't need it!" the soldier protested. He was a reservist going home.

"Then give it to the first soldier you see who does need it." He pushed the fifty shekels on the reservist. The reservist took the money.

"How'd you like a shwarma?" he asked two English speakers he recognized on the street. They looked hungry.

After he bought them shwarmas, Levi was walking home. "Do you want ten *mehadrin* frozen chickens?" a friend offered.

Hashem, thank you! Mr. Levi thought. *That's a really fast return of investment for two shwarmas."*

His second day back home Levi opened his shop. An American tourist came in.

"How's business?"

"It's bad. Really bad."

The tourist gave him $500 cash. Immediately Mr. Levi gave the *ma'aser* on the $500 to his employee. Levi felt terrible that he hadn't been able to pay him for a month.

The next day an American woman came into his shop.

"I have some *tzedakah* for families in the North. Does anybody need it?"

"My employee," Levi said. "I couldn't pay him during the whole war."

She gave his employee $300.

Two days later, the lady came back to Levi's shop. "I was thinking about how you put your employee before yourself," she said. "So I came back today with money for you, too." And she gave him another $300.

"G-d Will Help"

"**I** got the first urgent call a few days after the war started," said Rabbi Binyomin Rosenberg, director of Eizer L'Shabbos in Tzefat. "I realized that people were suffering. They had no money, no savings. People needed food. They couldn't wait for the donations to come in the mail. When you're hungry, every hour counts. I went to cash a personal check for $40,000 in Bnei Brak.

" 'But you don't have the money to cover it,' the man said to me.

" 'Don't worry, *G-tt vill helfen*.' I told him. 'G-d will help.'

"A little over a week later, the funds came in to cover my check. People heard what was going on here, and they started to give.

"*Rebbetzin* Elisheva Mirvis from Moshav S'dei Ilan is on the phone nonstop. All the money for the cooked food distributions from Eizer L' Shabbos is coming from her fund-raising. Everybody else's donations to Eizer L'Shabbos are covering the free groceries, the grocery store vouchers, and emergency cash for people to survive.

"I haven't said no to a single person who has turned to me for help," Rabbi Rosenberg said, "The people staying in Tzefat mostly need food. We give them either groceries or grocery vouchers. The people who left need money. People took very little with them. The end of the month is approaching, and people don't have rent money. People are calling me from all over the country."

"How much money do you need to keep this up if the war lasts a month?" I asked.

"Oh, about $250,000. *G-tt vill helfen*."

છ   છ   છ

Rabbi Simcha and Elisheva Mirvis live on Moshav S'dei Ilan, a half-hour south of Tzefat, where it was quiet at the beginning of the war (later they were under fire, too). Friends from Jerusalem called the *rabbanit*, wanting to know how they could help Tzefat. She contacted Rabbi Rosenberg, and he told her the people staying in Tzefat desperately needed cooked meals.

"I called Kibbutz Lavi to cater, because they had lost all of their tourist business. They asked me how I was going to pay for it. 'I don't know,' I told them. 'I'll make some phone calls.' She also posted it on their website.

"Hashem helped me. Sometimes it was so obvious. One Thursday evening in the middle of the war, we had six hundred catered Shabbat meals ready to deliver to Tzefat. I got a call: 'We need another 600 meals.'

"*Where am I going to get the money tonight?* I thought. *And who is going to cook them now, so close to Shabbat?*

"Radio Kol Chai called me just then. 'We heard about your fund-raising. We want to help.' I told them my dilemma. 'OK, in ten minutes you're on the air.'

"They raised 30,000 shekels in the next couple of hours. They just kept repeating the request over and over and people kept calling to give money. I called a Tiveria caterer. He woke up a few of his neighbors. They cooked all night and by 9 a.m. Friday morning, six hundred meals were ready to go to Tzefat.

"One Friday morning, five meals were left over. It seemed nobody in town wanted them. Exactly five soldiers came into Tzefat asking for *mehadrin* food for Shabbat.

"The first week, after Shabbat, a family staying in a bomb shelter in Tzefat called me to complain. They didn't get food from us, they got food from another distributor, and her children got sick. They had no more clean sheets, and the shelter was unlivable.

" 'You don't need food,' I told her. 'You need to get out of there. I'm sending you a van.' We picked up twenty-five people — nine children and eight grandchildren, and their parents — and sent them to Kibbutz Lavi. The driver said he wanted his family to stay there too, so they came. Kibbutz Lavi gave them free guest houses, clothes, three cooked meals a day, and did their laundry for four weeks."

"How much money did you raise during the war?"

"Five hundred thousand shekels. We expanded our help to Kiryat Shemona and Tiveria, so we were sending meals two to three times a week to three cities under attack.

Boundless Chesed

"How much money did you raise?" I asked Rabbanit Tova Eliyahu. Every time I stopped by, she was on the phone. I knew she was fund-raising for Tzefat emergency needs.

"Two hundred thousand shekels," she said.

"Where did it come from?"

"Most of it came from one Jewish family in Brazil. The rest came mostly from Jews and Christians in America. The rav gave most of it directly to private families, cash in their hand — all kinds of families, whoever needed it. He also gave a lot of money to *rabbanim* to give to their *kehillot*. They would know best who needs it the most."

Rav Mordechai Dov Kaplan, *rav* of the Old City, and *rosh ye-shivah* of the Yeshivah of Safed, worried about the working people who were suddenly in need. Working closely with Mateh Aharon, a Tzefat fund-raising organization, and the mayor, Rav Kaplan launched an emergency drive to get grocery money distributed to a thousand Tzefat families. The families on welfare are easy to find and thus easy to help. The families closely involved with the major shuls and yeshivahs can turn to their *rabbanim*. But what about the average working-class family that barely gets by during normal times? At the beginning of the war, the banks were closed. Many people wouldn't get paid for the duration of the war. He went out to find these families, to knock on their doors, and give each family a grocery voucher for three hundred shekels.

"That means you gave out three hundred thousand shekels worth of food coupons," I said.

"Yes, that's right."

The city had to rely on *chesed* organizations to provide most of the money needed for the food distributions. The army coordinated their delivery, using Livnot, Noam Fund, private Israeli citizens, and volunteers from abroad.

Chabad opened the soup kitchen, and Rabbi Marzel sent out food and gave out emergency cash at Beit Chabad. Noam Fund, Eizer L'Shabbos, and Lev U'Neshama, which provide Shabbos groceries year round, helped needy families.

Many dedicated Jews continued work in the hospital, the nursing home, the health clinics, and social services, as if there were no missiles flying overhead.

"Do you have any stories?" I asked a social worker in the nursing home.

" 'There is nothing to say,' she told me. 'We just did what needed to be done.' " Hanging on their bulletin board is a thank you letter from a grateful daughter whose aged mother, among other senior residents, was taken from her home to the nursing home for the course of the war.

The rabbinic families, organizations, and private citizens mentioned here are only a small fraction of those who dedicated their every waking hour and much of their nights' sleep to help the people of Tzefat survive. So many, many more did the same. Some don't want their names mentioned. Others' efforts weren't brought to my attention. And just as there are so many Tzefat people, so many Tzefat stories that are not represented here, the same is true of every town and moshav in Israel. *Am Yisrael* has a lot to be proud of.

CHANA BESSER

Missiles and Miracles

ach missile brought with it *nissim* and *nifla'os*. Many people
were often within a few feet, a few yards of each direct hit
in town. Each time, dozens of people were at risk of injury
from flying glass and shrapnel hurled at high speeds far away
from the point of impact in every direction. Yet few people were
seriously injured. Hundreds were struck with glass or shrapnel
fragments, and each one is a miracle story of how they were not
hurt more seriously, *chas v'shalom*. Most walked out of the hospital and resumed their normal activities the same day.

Most amazing of all, beyond all mathematical probability,
is how many of the missiles landed in fields, between houses, in
empty courtyards, or on empty roads and sidewalks. In a town
full of houses and buildings, this is an open miracle.

Rabbi Elazar Keonig, the well-respected Breslov Rav of Tzefat,
spoke to the women in town. He said, "*Kamah Hashem ohev otanu!*
How much Hashem loves us! Hundreds and hundreds of missiles
were aimed at us, and Hashem directed them again and again and
again so that most of the time no one was hurt."

Those missiles that struck houses usually exploded in an
empty room, often a room that someone had just left. In some instances, shrapnel from a direct hit just outside a room, flew over
or in front of someone, and lodged in a wall. More than once,
shrapnel flew into a room, bounced off a wall, and ricocheted

again through the room, leaving the people inside unhurt. We are able to tell only a few of the thousands of stories of Hashem's infinite kindness and mercy here. Even if we could collect every story from every eyewitness, how many more stories would be left unknown to us of hidden miracles and wonders unseen by mortal man.

The first day of the war
Thursday, July 13, 8 p.m.

Orly Shnor was inside her home on Bar Yochai Street with three of her daughters. Her neighbor Tzippy Rothenberg, was standing in her courtyard, speaking with her sister in America on her cordless phone.

"Here, I'll hold up the phone and you can hear the booms from Mount Meron," Tzippy told her sister. She held up her phone and shared the reality of Israel being at war with her sister.

Tzippy had invited Orly's two little girls to come to her house to play.

"They're still eating," Orly told her, "and they're afraid to leave the house by themselves with the booms. Do you want to come get them?"

"No problem," Tzippy answered and continued to talk to her sister while she waited for the two girls, ages six and three, in the courtyard.

Now Orly was talking on the phone, too, with her teenage son who was away in yeshivah. "Let me take the phone out into the courtyard and you'll hear the booms coming from Mount Meron," she told her son as she walked down the four steps from her dining room toward her courtyard door. Orly was standing by the door about to open it, but a voice in her head told her, "No. He'll hear better from the back window."

Meanwhile, Tzippy left the courtyard and brought the two little girls into her house across the cobblestone path. She was still on the phone with her sister when the missile exploded — smack in the middle of the courtyard she had just left.

Tzippy's door was open. People out on the street ran into her house for safety. Children screamed. Windows broke.

Orly's teenage daughter came running for her sisters, relieved that they had made it safely into their neighbor's house. Assured that her children and neighbors were safe, that no one on the street was hurt, Orly ran to put out the fires in her courtyard. A sofa and other things were burning. Pieces of the roof of her shed and branches from a nearby tree were everywhere.

"Where did the missile explode?" Orly's husband, Ofir, was in shul when the missile exploded in the Old City. He couldn't reach his wife, so he called his daughter. Tzippy answered his daughter's cell phone.

"Everyone's fine.'

"What do you mean, everyone's fine? Where did the missile explode?"

"Everyone's fine and it hit your courtyard."

The missile had taken a good portion off the top of a tree near the courtyard. The tree had deflected it. If it hadn't hit the tree, the natural course of the missile would have brought it down either into the house on Bar Yochai Street, on the sidewalk where six people were walking, or perhaps into Tzippy's house.

Orly had always hated that tree. It blocked her mountain view and made a mess in her courtyard. But Keren Kayemet considered it an old tree worth preserving and so they had given up on getting rid of it. "Only Hashem knew a year ago that the tree had to be standing there today to save our lives," Orly said.

In a house near the Shnors' courtyard, a neighbor had been cooking in her kitchen for a few hours. A moment before the missile struck, she had suddenly left the kitchen. Just after she left the room, her kitchen window shattered with tremendous impact. She was safely in the next room.

"By the way, did you latch the gate?" Orly asked Tzippy three weeks later.

"I don't remember. Why?"

"Because two teenage girls were on the street. They heard the whistle of the missile coming down overhead, and they tried to run into my courtyard for safety, but the gate was latched and they couldn't open it quickly enough. So they ran into the corner on the street outside my courtyard. You know, where the courtyard is further out toward the street than my house. The window over their heads was the only window in my house that didn't break. If that gate would have been open..."

First day of the war, Kiryat Breslov

"The first miracle," said Adele, "is that all the kids were safely in their own homes, because it was a fast day so school was dismissed early."

Midafternoon she heard a missile whistling its ominous warning above her roof. Adele grabbed her children and immediately put them into the safe room in their house. There was a knock at her door. A family of eleven stood there, crying and frightened. They were out-of-towners, visiting the *kivrei tzaddikim* in the famous Tzefat cemetery, caught unawares by the first missiles of the war. They stayed for two hours and then took a cab home.

That night, other families started calling. These were friends, members of their *kehillah*. "The Rav says we should ask to stay with you," each family told them. One said, "We don't have a safe room." Another said, "Our children are scared." By the time Shabbos came in, they were hosting four families, a total of seventeen people. They stayed for a whole month, for the duration of the war. Another six neighborhood kids came by every day to join in the children's activities, and three of them slept over because their families' safe rooms weren't big enough for their large families.

More families came and left occasionally. Rav Koenig sent food, and the women cooked in Adele's big Pesach pots. They divided up the house into a ladies' and small children section and a men's section.

The first Shabbos of the war, the Rav performed a bris at the shul and everyone went. At the *kiddush* after the bris, the Rav spoke. "Now a time has come, not a simple time..." From this Adele understood that this would not be a quick war. It would not be over in a day or two, or in a week or two.

Wow, Adele thought. *It's a big responsibility to have all these people in our house. Maybe they should leave Tzefat? Maybe we should leave Tzefat?* She called the Rav early Sunday morning. "I'm afraid to stay. I don't know if it's safe."

"You have a good house," the Rav told Adele. "You have the *zechus* to have a good house and to have these people staying by you." He gave her advice to ensure their safety. "Don't speak too much — don't speak *devarim beteilim*. Study *hilchos Shabbos* and *shemiras halashon*. Pray for all of the soldiers and for all who left Tzefat." The Rav told her husband not to go outside and to keep the kids inside.

So, armed with the Rav's advice, they organized activities for the children and Torah learning for the adults. They ran a day camp for the girls in the house. The boys were escorted daily to a temporary, nearby cheder where they learned and played for three hours in the morning and two and a half hours in the evening.

The Katyusha miracles happened about a week after they spoke with their *rav*.

It was early in the afternoon. Adele saw her neighbor in the front yard with her two children and invited her in to eat something. Then she took the laundry to the front yard to hang it outside.

Meanwhile, in a nearby house, a boy went to make a cup of coffee for his father. When he looked out the window, he saw his two rebbes who were teaching him in the temporary cheder. They were headed toward a shortcut up the steep hillside, a crudely constructed narrow ledge of steppingstones used by all, including the Tzefat mailmen. "Come through here," the boy called. "I have the keys to the building." The rebbes changed their course and walked toward the boy's house instead.

That's when the missile struck, exploding on the stone stairway up the hillside. The two rebbes had just enough time to throw themselves over the threshold of the boy's doorway, pushed to the floor by the impact of the explosion.

The blast caught Adele outside hanging her laundry, pushed her down and nailed her to the floor. For a while, she couldn't hear. The courtyard was full of gunpowder. Metal, stones, and wood flew all around her. The first few minutes Adele said only *"Shema Yisrael..."* again and again. In her heart she said, *Please, Hashem, I want to see everybody alive here. I don't mind if I lose my hearing. Just let me see that everybody is alive.* Nothing touched her. She was unhurt.

About twenty people were close by. There were men working on a construction project outdoors. Shrapnel entered houses and whipped around at high speeds. Five children were playing on the family's second balcony, on the other side of the house away from the explosion. No one was injured, not even a scratch.

A few seconds later, two more missiles exploded on the other side of the house, about ten yards from the balcony on the side where the children were playing. Only soft clumps of dirt flew onto the children.

Exactly the place where these two missiles exploded had been a large underground gas tank which had supplied the whole community. Half a year before, the gas company had come and taken it away. The residents couldn't understand why the gas company had done that, why they didn't want to do business with them anymore. And everyone had been inconvenienced. Each family had to order and install their own private, family-size gas tanks. Now they saw that it had saved them from a massive gas explosion today.

In one home a man was standing in his kitchen, directly in front of his kitchen window, when the last two missiles struck. The whole kitchen window exploded, glass went all around him, his roof collapsed above him, red particles of clay everywhere mixed with the glass. Another window in his house melted from the heat of the explosion. He stood there in the middle of it all, untouched and unharmed.

The police and army arrived immediately and couldn't believe that everyone was all right. It took an hour or so before everyone grasped how dangerous it truly had been, and how many miracles had happened that day.

"You had a big miracle," the Rav told the family. "You all need to make a seudah to give thanks to Hashem and *bentch gomel* early tomorrow morning."

That night, Adele couldn't sleep at all. She spoke to the Rav late the next morning.

"Rav, I can't sleep!"

"Fear is not so bad for a person. You can use it for good. It can break the azus of the guf. '*Shema Yisrael Hashem Elokeinu Hashem Echad*' — these six words are our six cities of refuge. If someone is afraid, they can leave. We will find them a place to go."

After hearing that, Adele slept soundly. Adele had told herself, *Don't worry. You are in Tzefat. Don't worry. Even the air here protects us.*

"We did leave — for two days," Adele said, "and all I wanted was to go back home. I felt that Tzefat was the safest place."

RABBI DOVID HELLER

Finishing the Job

From a devar Torah given in Tzefat on Shabbos parashas Re'eh, August 19, 2006, the first Shabbos after the cease-fire went into effect.

S omeone remarked to me that it's a shame that the Israel Defense Forces weren't allowed to totally destroy the Hez- bollah and their infrastructure. I reflected that all the wars that I remember since the establishment of the State of Israel seem to have the same theme: The Arabs would pose a serious threat to the safety and existence of the Jews here in Israel. Then Israel would be forced into a war with them and would triumph, but not be allowed to finish the job, thus leaving the potential threat still simmering.

We have a facsimile to this pattern in the Torah itself. In *para-shas Beshalach (Shemos* 17:13), the Torah states that Yehoshua weakened Amalek. Rashi brings the *Midrash Tanchuma* that states that Yehoshua killed Amalek's strong ones and left only the weak ones and that he did so at the command of Hashem.

I find this midrash difficult to understand. In the next three *pesukim* Hashem tells Moshe Rabbeinu that He will surely eradi- cate even the remembrance of Amalek and that there is to be a continual war against them for all times. Rashi says that Hashem takes an oath that He will make war and animosity against Amalek forever. Hashem's Throne will not be complete until Amalek is totally annihilated. My question: Why did Hashem wait? Why not allow Yehoshua to finish the job?

My answer comes from Rashi. Rashi (on *Shemos* 17:8) brings the example of a child whose father carries him on his shoulders and does the child's bidding again and again. Then they encounter an acquaintance, and the child (while sitting on the fathers shoulders) asks the acquaintance if he knows where his father is. The father says rhetorically, "You don't know where I am?" He sets the child down on the road and along comes a dog and bites him.

So, too, Hashem took *klal Yisrael* out of Mitzrayim and drowned the Egyptians in the sea and sustained the Jews miraculously in the desert, and still they tested Hashem to see if He was in their midst. Thus he lowered His protection — and along came Amalek.

So the appearance of Amalek, whom the Torah states must be permanently eradicated, was caused by the Jews' testing Hashem. We feel that we have the right to test Him by doing what we want and not doing His will for us. As long as we individually or collectively retain this attitude, we will have to suffer the afflictions of the external Amalek.

It is not the Israel Defense Forces that must finish the job, but each and every one of us. And no one is stopping us but ourselves.

Date: September 21, 2006
From: Chana Besser
To: Tzefat under Fire list
Subject: A New Year blessing

Dear Family and Friends,

This is the strangest High Holiday season. They say that in Shamayim everything is upside down from the way we perceive it in this world. (Actually, it's this world that is upside down — Shamayim is the world of truth.) Well, the war turned my holidays upside down this year.

My Elul was sitting in the bomb shelter the first two days of the war. My Rosh HaShanah was the first Shabbos under fire. The whole war was my Aseres Yemei Teshuvah. My Yom Kippur was the day that the closest Katyusha blasted through all my klippahs. And everybody coming home was my Sukkas. Nobody believed by then that the walls of our houses were any more protection than the flimsy walls of our sukkahs.

Leah Golomb taught this Torah from the Slonimer Rebbe: The geulah for klal Yisrael will come as each and every Jew goes through his personal geulah. And so I bless you and your loved ones with your own personal geulah. I bless you to light up your "os" in Hashem's Torah with such a pure candle that it never goes out. I bless you that you should have the greatest joy and nachas in the new year.

Kesivah v'chasimah tovah and a wonderful New Year,
chana

I Am Thankful To...

I am thankful to HaKadosh Baruch Hu for giving me life and health and His *hashgachah pratis* that brought about this book, Faith under Fire. He guided me to my Rebbe, Rav Mordechai Twerski, *shlita*, the Hornosteipeler Rebbe, whom I want to thank for his encouragement and advice and for reviewing this book and contributing a *devar Torah*.

Those who enjoy this book have Rebbetzin Tziporah Heller to thank because it was her idea. I am grateful to Rebbetzin Heller for taking the time to review it, contribute to it, and make it a reality.

I deeply appreciate the *mesiras nefesh* of Avraham Sutton and Kezia Pride, who interrupted their own projects and commitments to make *Faith under Fire* possible.

Those who enjoy the variety of stories and letters in this book can join me in thanking the contributing writers. Those who enjoy my stories can join me in thanking the Tzefas Women Writers' Group, founded by Esther Heller. They help me develop my strengths, overcome my weaknesses, and celebrate my successes as if they are their own. I especially want to thank the people who submitted excellent stories and graciously forgave us when we couldn't publish them all.

It is an honor to work with Targum Press. From the beginning, I have appreciated their integrity, their professionalism, and their sensitivity. I especially want to thank Miriam Zakon and Suri Brand for the extra time and enthusiasm they have devoted to *Faith under Fire*. I'm grateful to Diane Liff for making the photos a memorable part of this book and for the layout and cover design.

I want to thank all those who contributed the outstanding photos, especially professional photographers Eliyahu Alpern and Shmuel Aharon Rockwerk.

Most authors thank their immediate family for their self-sacrifice. My daughters and sister live on another continent, but if they were living with me, they would have earned such praise. I thank them for their encouragement and support.

Many more people helped with a variety of needs and even more offered to help. I am grateful to all who helped to make this book possible, to all who offered to help, and to all who encouraged me during the process. I share the celebration and the *simchah* of bringing *Faith under Fire* to press with everyone named above and anyone not named above.

My greatest desire and my goal from the beginning is that *Faith under Fire* will help to reveal Hashem's Awesome and Holy Name.

Glossary

"Ani Ma'amin" — literally, "I believe"; the first words of each of the thirteen principles of faith

achdus — unity

aliyah — spiritual ascent of a soul after a person's death; term used to describe immigration to Israel

am Yisrael — the Jewish nation

b'ezras Hashem — "with the help of G-d"

ba'al teshuvah — penitent; returnee to the Jewish faith

baruch Dayan ha'emes — "blessed is the true Judge [G-d]," said after hearing of a death

bentch — bless

berachah — blessing

bitachon — faith

bli ayin hara — literally, "no evil eye"; phrase said to ward off the evil eye

Chazal — Talmudic Sages

cheder — boys' elementary school

chesed — acts of kindness; good deeds

chizuk — encouragement; inspiration

da'as Torah — Torah authority

daven — pray

devar Torah — literally, "word of Torah"; brief discourse on a Torah topic

emunah — belief

erev Shabbos — Friday; the day before Shabbos

gabbai — curator of a synagogue

gadol — leading Torah sage of the generation

galus — exile

geulah — redemption

go'el tzedek — the righteous redeemer

gomel — blessing said after surviving a dangerous situation

hafrashas challah — the mitzvah of separating a small piece of dough when making challah, traditionally to be given to a Jewish priest (*kohen*), but today destroyed, usually burned

haftorah — portion of Prophets or Writings read in the synagogue on Sabbath after the Torah reading

halachah — Jewish law

hamotzi — blessing said before eating bread

hashgachah pratis— divine providence

hesder — program in which boys combine regular Torah study with army service

hishtadlus — effort

Kabbalas Shabbos — prayer said at the commencement of the Sabbath

kavanah — concentration; intent when praying or making a blessing

kehillah — community

kever — grave; tomb

kibbud av va'em — honoring one's parents

Kiddush — blessing over wine said on the Sabbath

kiddush Hashem — sanctification of G-d's Name

kippah — yarmulke; head covering worn by Jewish men

klal Yisrael — the Jewish people

kollel — a place where married men learn Torah all day and receive a small stipend

levayah — funeral

ma'aser — tithe; a tenth of one's income given to charity

Mashiach — Messiah

mekubal — an expert in Kabbalah

mesiras nefesh — self-sacrifice

middos — character traits

motza'ei Shabbos — Saturday night

nachas — pleasure; usually associated with achievements of a child or student

navi — prophet

neshamah — soul

niftar — passed away

niggun — tune; melody

Olam Haba — the World to Come

Olam Hazeh — this world

oneg Shabbos — enjoyment of the Sabbath

parashah — Torah portion

parnasah — livelihood

pasuk — verse

posek; poskim — halachic authority; decisor in Jewish law

rabbanim — rabbis

rav — rabbi

Rebbe — sage and spiritual leader; teacher

rebbetzin — the wife of a rabbi

rosh yeshivah — the head of a yeshivah

sefer — book

sefer Torah — Torah scroll

sefirot — literally, "spheres"; the channels by which G-d sends His bounty

segulah — spiritual remedy

seudah — meal

shalom bayis — harmony in the home

shehecheyanu — a blessing of renewal and gratitude recited at ordained times

Shemoneh Esrei — silent prayer recited three times daily

shidduch — date

shiur — Torah lecture

shivah — seven-day mourning period after the death of a close relative

shul — synagogue

siddur — prayer book

simchah — joy

siyum — celebration upon completing a portion of the Torah or Talmud

tafkid — mission; task

Talmud Torah — an elementary school for boys

tefillah — prayer

Tefillas HaDerech — prayer said when traveling

Tehillim — Psalms

teshuvah — repentance

Tishah B'Av — Ninth of Av, the saddest day of the Jewish calendar

Tu B'Av — the fifteenth of Av, traditionally a day of joy

tzaddik — righteous person

tzedakah — charity

tznius — modesty

yahrtzeit — anniversary of a death

yishuv — settlement

z"l — acronym for "*zichrono livrachah*," may his memory be blessed

zechus — merit

zemiros — songs sung on the Sabbath, usually at meals

zt"l — acronym for "*zecher tzaddik livrachah*," may the memory of this righteous person be blessed